Manufacturing Solutions for Consistent Quality & Reliability

Manufacturing Solutions for Consistent Quality & Reliability

The Nine-Step Problem-Solving Process

Robert W. Traver

amacom

American Management Association

New York • Boston • Chicago • Kansas City • San Francisco • Washington, D.C.
Brussels • Mexico City • Tokyo • Toronto

This book is available at a special
discount when ordered in bulk quantities.
For information, contact Special Sales Department,
AMACOM, a division of American Management Association,
135 West 50th Street, New York, NY 10020.

This publication is designed to provide accurate and authoritative information in regard to the subject matter covered. It is sold with the understanding that the publisher is not engaged in rendering legal, accounting, or other professional service. If legal advice or other expert assistance is required, the services of a competent professional person should be sought.

Library of Congress Cataloging-in-Publication Data

Traver, Robert W.
    Manufacturing solutions for consistent quality & reliability /
Robert W. Traver.
       p. cm.
    Includes bibliographical references and index.
    ISBN 0-8144-0271-2 (acid-free paper)
    1. Quality control—Case studies. 2. Reliability (Engineering)—
Case studies. 3. Problem solving. I. Title.
TS156.T73   1995
658.5'62—dc20
                                   94-46901
                                       CIP

Printing number

10 9 8 7 6 5 4 3 2 1

This book is dedicated to
Valarie, my wife,
for her cheerful typing of the many
revisions of the material and the plotting
and replotting of the numerous figures.

Contents

Foreword by H. James Harrington, Principal,
Ernst & Young   *ix*

Preface   *xiii*

Acknowledgment   *xvii*

  1   Key Variable Isolation   1

  2   Multi-Vari Studies   7

  3   Quantification: The Initial Diagnostic Step   13

  4   The Case of Out-of-Specification Coil Resistance   18

  5   Interactions   22

  6   The Case of the Flat Beer
      by John M. Reddy   25

  7   Designed Experiments   32

  8   The Case of Porous Decorative Rings   38

  9   The Case of Scrapped Artillery Projectiles   46

10   The Case of Shorts on Dust Cover Seals   55

11   The Case of Rejects on a Multicavity Compression
      Molder   61

12   The Case of Varying Seat Measurements   66

13   The Case of Bore Defects on Centrifugal Castings   74

14   The Case of Weeping Stoppers   82
      by Thomas S. Woods

15 Introduction to Isoplots   91

16 The Case of the Noisy Motor   102
        by Art Leason

17 The Case of Low Yield on Solid-State Devices   112
        by John Pollard and John M. Reddy

18 The Case of Improving Aluminum Die-Casting
        Quality   123
        by Robert W. Traver With Gregory Brown

19 The Case of Nondisintegrating Tablets   140
        by Charles L. Rosen

20 The Case of the Eccentric Discs   150

21 The Case of the Spline Demerits   155

22 The Case of the Mysterious Hot Crank   160

23 Variables Search   174

24 Parallel Path Experimentation   183

Epilogue   187

Appendixes: Multi-Vari Exercises   189

Appendix I. Rope Consistency   191

Appendix II. Foundry Measles Charts   201

Glossary   213

Bibliography   221

Index   223

Foreword

Everyone talks about industrial problem solving and some books explain how to do it. These books typically provide precise methods for selecting the problem to work on and ways to protect customers from receiving defective products. The instructions often are to not treat the symptoms, but to define the root cause so that the real problem can be corrected. It sounds so simple. All you have to do is define the root cause — but these books never tell you how. Why do they avoid giving details about this crucial activity? The reason is simple. Defining the root cause is very difficult and complex, and they don't have a good way of finding the cause that works all the time.

There are a number of ways to get to the root of an industrial problem. A good failure analysis laboratory can provide the insight necessary to understand how a failure such as a broken bolt occurred. Duplicating the failure under laboratory conditions also has proven an effective way to define the root cause of problems. Each of these approaches works well, but they require expensive laboratories and highly trained personnel.

Excessive variation is at the heart of most problems, at least the difficult ones. Variation is part of life. No two items or acts are exactly identical. Even identical twins have very different fingerprints, voice patterns, and personal values. No two screws made on the same machine are exactly the same. Equipment may not be sensitive enough to measure the variation, but it exists. Some variation is good. It keeps our lives from being monotonous. No one would like steak, mashed potatoes, and peas three times a day, every day of the week. They are good for a special treat, but would get old and boring if eaten at every meal.

Some variation—within specific limits—has little or no effect on output. In other cases, variation can cause an entire plant to come to a halt. The variation we're concerned about here is the variation that causes problems resulting in waste. There is no such thing as a random problem, just problems whose occurrence is more or less infrequent—meaning that the combination of specific variables occurs more or less infrequently. The art of defining the root cause is the art of variables analysis and isolation.

The root cause of a problem has been found when the key variables that caused the problem have been isolated. Over the years, there have been many methods developed to isolate key variables. Designed experiments and Taguchi methods are popular today. But the difficulties and effort required to prepare and conduct these studies cause them to be used on only a small fraction of the problems. Engineers, managers, production employees, and sales personnel solve most of their problems by brute force and a lot of luck. Even then, most of the time the answer that is implemented is not the best solution to the problem.

At last, a simple but effective way of systematically looking at and understanding variation has been developed—key variable isolation using multi-vari. This technique unlocks the door and shows users how to interpret the clues that solve even the most difficult problems. Key variable isolation using multi-vari provides a systematic approach that can unlock the mysteries of variation. By studying different types of variation, the source of the variation can be identified. Then the problem solver can quickly and effectively reduce the many potential sources to a critical few and often to a single factor, thereby greatly simplifying the problem evaluation cycle and reducing the amount of data for collection. The results can be outstanding:

- Problems can be solved faster.
- Fewer samples are required.
- Less-skilled people can solve very complex problems.
- Preventive and corrective action plans can be evaluated quickly.

• Nontechnical people can easily understand the results of a technical evaluation.

The techniques defined in this book are not new and untried. They are based on more than three decades of successful practical experience by a group of highly skilled consultants and their clients. The book is particularly helpful because it presents theory and then provides detailed case histories that describe exactly how the theory is applied. The presentation of this valuable material is enhanced by the wealth of knowledge and practical experience that Robert Traver and his associates have accumulated throughout the years.

H. James Harrington
Principal, Ernst & Young
Former President and Chairman of the Board, ASQC

Preface

With the increasing emphasis on quality in American industry, numerous books have been written on many aspects of product and service quality. Some of these books focus on statistical process control and/or statistical concepts, while many others emphasize the importance of senior management commitment, involvement, participation, and support. This emphasis on senior management commitment is sound, because without it quality programs would prove unsuccessful or at best short-lived. Many of these management-oriented books also stress quality systems—which mean open-ended and on-going processes, rather than closed-ended programs.

Manufacturing Solutions for Consistent Quality & Reliability stresses problem solving as a system for continuous improvement and does not merely present statistical concepts or describe statistical process control (SPC). The book emphasizes the use of graphical analysis in problem solving because it is straightforward and far easier to interpret and implement than complex statistical methods.

Graphical analysis is at the heart of the multi-vari problem-solving strategy of key variable isolation, which is the focus of the book. Multi-vari identifies which variables and/or interactions are causing quality problems and then guides you to the elimination of the problem and control of the variables. Production then becomes more consistent and less sensitive to outside influences.

From the 1950s through the early 1970s a group of management consultants under Dorian Shainin at Rath & Strong, Inc., used this problem-solving strategy under the name *statistical engineering* to solve engineering and manufacturing problems. After a time this title was replaced by the term *variation research*. Later, I felt that the word *research* could be misleading so I modified the term to *variables isolation*. It seemed an apt title because the task is always to isolate the variable(s) or interaction of variables that causes problems.

The problem-solving strategy of what I now call *key variable isolation* is not a fancy name for statistical methods nor is it an alternative to classical statistical methods. Instead, it incorporates these techniques when they are appropriate. Key variable isolation has its own set of methods and procedures. The case histories in this book illustrate these methods and procedures. While some of these case histories share significant similarities, others are more unique. Therefore, the common approach used throughout the book may escape the notice of the more casual reader. The Traver Nine-Step Problem-Solving Process shown in Figure 1 provides the common thread throughout each case history. The industrial investigator(s) used this process though many cases required fewer than the full nine steps. Nevertheless, the process provides a guide or track to the investigators.

An important element of key variable isolation is the multi-vari study, which reveals clues to the cause of the problem. Although different names can be attached to some specific techniques, the real strength of key variable isolation lies in the integration of old and new methods into a realistic problem-solving strategy.

Anyone involved in reducing product variation, improving consistency, and reducing the incidence of defective products and the related costs of poor quality will benefit from this book. In particular, process, manufacturing, product, industrial, and quality control/assurance engineers should find the concepts important and useful. All management in the manufacturing sector should also become familiar with the key variable isolation strategy so that they can recognize situations where its application would be beneficial.

Using key variable isolation as the way to locate the key variable(s) goes a long way toward realizing Walter Shewhart's of Bell Laboratories classic statement, "The long-range contribution of statistics depends not so much upon getting a lot of highly trained statisticians into industry, as it does in creating

Figure 1. The Traver Nine-Step Problem Process Reducing Variability—Isolating the Key Variables.

1. **PROVIDE FOCUS** *Determine Importance of Problem*
   1. Quality Costs
   2. Pareto Analyses
   3. p Charts
   4. Check Sheets
   5. Histograms
   6. Corrective Action Reports
   7. Customer Surveys
   8. Customer Complaints
   9. Warranty Costs
2. **GET CLOSE TO THE PROBLEM** *See What Is Really Going On*
3. **QUANTIFY THE OUTPUT** *Develop a Variable Scale (If None Exists)*
   1. Measurement Capability
   2. 0–5 Scale
   3. Jury Panels
4. **RUN MULTI-VARI STUDY(IES)** *"Let the Process Do the Talking"*
   1. Multi-Vari Studies
      a. Visual Analysis
      b. Patterns of Variation
      c. Nonrandom Patterns and Differences
   2. Measles Charts
5. **DESIGN EXPERIMENT(S)** *Test the Variables for Causes and Effects*
   1. Full Factorials
   2. Variables Search
   3. Component Search
   4. Parallel Path Experimentation
   5. Random and Multiple Balance
   6. Fractional Factorials
6. **TURN THE PROBLEM ON AND OFF** *Prove You Have the Answer*
7. **OPTIMIZE** *Run Tests with Proven Variables*
   1. Designed Experiments—Multi Level
   2. EVOP
   3. REVOP
8. **INSTALL PROCESS CONTROLS ON KEY VARIABLE(S)** *Use Most Cost-Effective Tool*
   1. Precontrol
   2. Median Charts
   3. $\overline{X}$-R Charts
   4. p Charts
9. **MEASURE BEFORE AND AFTER RESULTS** *Quantify Continuous Improvement*
   1. Dollars
   2. Quality Costs
   3. Scrap Costs
   4. Rework Costs
   5. Customer Complaints
   6. Warranty Costs

a statistically minded generation of physicists, chemists, engineers, and others who will . . . have a hand in developing and directing the production processes of tomorrow." Perhaps even more to the point: employees do not have to become statisticians—they need to learn how to apply basic statistical concepts as tools to solve industrial problems.

Five of my present and past associates at Reddy, Traver & Woods, Inc., have contributed to this book to ensure that a broad range of industries would be covered. I am grateful to them for their input and support.

R. W. T.

Acknowledgment

It was only through the patient editing of my daughter, Elizabeth Traver, that a mass of jottings was converted into a readable book.

Manufacturing Solutions for Consistent Quality & Reliability

Chapter 1
Key Variable Isolation

Designed experiments and other statistical concepts have been making a positive contribution to American industry for many decades. However, the applications of these concepts during this time have differed greatly in various industries, and even within the same company. Unfortunately, the gap between theory and the actual application of these concepts on the factory floor has often remained too wide.

In contrast to highly structured statistical techniques, key variable isolation interweaves engineering, manufacturing, and statistical work so tightly that precise delineation is not possible. Investigative procedures such as detective work and key variable isolation contain both deductive and inductive aspects. One can learn the deductive aspects of detective work, such as fingerprinting or ballistics, from a book. Inductive skills, however, are much more difficult to acquire, and practice is needed to learn how to leap from clues to conclusion. Inductive skills may not be documentable or even teachable, and thus it may not be possible to write a recipe approach to either detective work or key variable isolation. It is possible, however, to explain the strategy and methods behind key variable isolation and to illustrate these methods with a series of case histories. This approach enables problem solvers to begin to acquire the skills necessary to use key variable isolation and to understand the wide range of its applicability.

Wherever these techniques are introduced, some initially doubt that the consultants and their programs can help because, "These outsiders don't understand our problems." But key variable isolation programs are always joint programs in which consultants work very closely with the technical people. Key variable isolation uses the technical knowledge in each industry because the consultants cannot apply these strategies in a vacuum. They depend on specific technical input from the client's technical personnel. Effective practitioners of key variable isolation draw on this technical expertise to help determine ways to quantify product defectiveness if no numerical scale exists; to design the tests; to iron out the problems of how to run tests; and to interpret the meaning of the data and conclusions. It is the insightful evaluation of the patterns of variation in the data that allows problem solvers to leap ahead to the next step using inductive reasoning. Key variable isolation techniques do not replace engineering judgment and manufacturing know-how—they enhance them. The engineer who has learned to use the key variable isolation tools becomes far more effective and valuable.

While every company is unique, problems are not. The advantage of the key variable isolation view of manufacturing problems is that the strategy can be applied to any industrial situation. Each problem is viewed from the standpoint of patterns of variation, and each successive test brings the investigator closer to the solution.

Process and Product

All manufacturing processes vary and, as a result, so do the products made by those processes. Generally, variation within specified limits is considered normal and acceptable. But sometimes the physical dimensions, performance characteristics, or visual appearance of a product will exceed the allowable limits; such product is often referred to as being defective.* The goal of modern manufacturing is to prevent defective products from being made in the first place. In real life, however, defective products are occasionally made, even

---

*The term *defective* will be applied to any product that does not meet specified requirements in one or more ways. Generally, the distinction will not be made as to whether such product is "fit to use," whether it can be reworked or salvaged, or whether it must be scrapped.

by processes that have been running a long time and from which all the bugs were thought to have been removed.

It is generally accepted that product defects are caused by one or more process input variables that are not performing properly. In this book, the term **key variable** (or **key process variable**) refers to the process input variable(s) that must be corrected or adjusted before the product made by the process can meet all the specified requirements. Process input variables, such as mold temperature, machine speed, raw material composition, air pressure, and operator techniques, become key variables when they cause or contribute to product problems.

Modern companies use many sources of information in order to determine whether there are problems with their products. Among the more common outside sources are customer complaints, warranty claims, and salespeople's reports. Inside sources might include total quality assurance audits, quality control studies (including Shewhart X-bar and R charts), and scrap and rework reports. However, in most cases determining that there is a problem is the easiest part. The hard part is to determine what is causing the problem. In this book the technique for determining the cause of product problems is referred to as **key variable isolation**—the series of techniques that determine which process variables contribute to or are responsible for defective products.

Key variable isolation makes no prior assumptions as to which process variable(s) is (are) responsible for problems in manufactured product. Instead, the process usually begins by sampling and inspecting the products being produced. The results of the inspection are then graphed, plotted, or otherwise analyzed using a technique called a **multi-vari study.** This analysis of the data inevitably rules out some process variables as the causes of product problems and often suggests other process variables. The step-by-step identification of types or patterns of variation is used to progressively reduce the field of process variables that might be causing the problem. Ultimately, only those process variables that are likely to be the source of the problem will remain to be studied further.

Comparing Approaches

Traditional Approach

The traditional engineering approach to problem solving provides solutions to many quality problems and involves the following steps:

1. Observe.
2. Think.
3. Try.
4. Explain.

In other words, an industrial investigator—when confronted with a manufacturing quality problem such as a physical defect or an out-of-tolerance dimension—will first *observe* the problem. Then, he or she will *think* of what process variable might be causing the problem. For example, is the pressure too high, the temperature too low, the time too long, the coolant not right, or the raw material out of specification? Next, he or she will *try* something, such as adjusting the process variable thought to be the cause of the problem to see if that will solve the problem. If the problem seems to disappear, the investigator might *explain* the solution as follows: the temperature was too low; the temperature was then increased, and now the process works properly.

Some quality problems of a general nature can be resolved simply by involving the workers. Brainstorming can also be useful in solving problems. However, when a difficult problem does not yield to the traditional engineering approach, employee involvement, or brainstorming, management may purchase expensive manufacturing equipment, select a different method of manufacturing, eliminate the product from the product line, accept the reduced quality, or design around the problem.

All of these options are costly and usually are chosen because the real cause of the product problem—that is, the key process variable (or variables)—has not been identified. Key variable isolation is one way to approach apparently unsolvable problems. Key process variable isolation using multi-vari, which yields a rapid convergence toward problem solution, is a systematic way of "listening" to a manufacturing process.

Key Variable Isolation Approach

The power and efficiency of the key variable isolation approach lie in its capacity to focus an investigation on one part of a complete manufacturing process and its product. This framing or bracketing often results in an elimination of one or more process variables that were previously thought to have a major impact on the product but are then found to have insignificant influence. Thus, the industrial investigator can focus on the aspects of the manufacturing operation that are most likely to be responsible for product problems.

Key variable isolation may be characterized as:

- A form of industrial detective work in which the investigator asks open-ended questions about the product and the process
- A strategy using unusual combinations of statistical methods
- The application of statistical methods, engineering judgment, manufacturing know-how, and common sense to solve the problem at hand

Key variable isolation uses techniques such as multi-vari analysis and designed experimentation along with numerical rating scales, measles charts, overstress testing, component search, variables search, and other analytic methods to determine the cause of product problems.

Learning the Methods

Key variable isolation is best learned through training under the *internship* method. A number of years ago a study determined the factors that produced the best surgeons. The study concluded that the only significant factor was the amount of time the prospective surgeon spent under the watchful eye and careful guidance of a successful surgeon acting as a coach, that is, through internship. While it is true that people do learn from their mistakes, they learn far more rapidly and efficiently by doing things right the first time. The experienced practitioner contributes to the learning process by coaching the proper methods.

Key variable isolation may be taught in a classroom situation. Solving real-life problems, however, requires a major leap from classroom training. Therefore, in addition to theory, case histories may be presented to help personnel understand how key variable isolation has actually been used. People often find that their specific problems are similar to those presented in a case history and can better learn by comparing the two situations.

After the case histories have been studied, trainees may be given hypothetical situations and asked to solve problems for which there may be a number of solutions. Typically, the classroom is divided into teams of three to five people for this problem-solving exercise. In a larger class the problems may be assigned to more than one team. Appendixes I and II present two hypothetical problems, followed by their solutions, that can be used to introduce the concepts of key variable isolation to company personnel.

Chapter 2

Multi-Vari Studies

The multi-vari technique is an integral part of the key variable isolation strategy. Multi-vari helps the industrial investigator to efficiently narrow the field of process input variables that may be causing problems in a product. The first published material on the multi-vari concept was written by L. A. Seder ("Diagnosis with Diagrams," *Industrial Quality Control*, Jan. 1950). Leonard Seder had been using this concept for a few years before the article was published.

Multi-vari begins with a stratified sampling and inspection of products being produced by the manufacturing process. The inspection results are then graphed, plotted, or otherwise analyzed. From a systematic analysis of the inspection results the investigator can determine the patterns of variation that are occurring in the process. A study might reveal, for example, that significant variation is occurring from shift to shift in a plastic injection molding operation; pieces produced during the first shift are greatly different from pieces produced during the second shift. This information allows the investigator to focus attention on the process input variables that can cause such variation. At the same time, the investigator can eliminate from consideration any variable that could not cause shift-to-shift variation. In this way, the investigator ultimately can identify the variable(s) that is causing the product problem (i.e., the investigator can isolate the *key* variable or variables). For example, if the same bag of plastic raw material was used during both shifts of the plastic injection molding operation it is unlikely that raw material composition is the key variable. If, however, a new lot of raw material was started at the beginning of the second shift, raw material composition could well be the key process variable.

The multi-vari technique may seem elementary, but is in fact a powerful tool. Many industrial problems go unsolved for long periods of time because in the "Think" step of the traditional engineering approach an incorrect assumption leads the investigation in the wrong direction. In multi-vari, however, the investigation is confined to process variables that fit the clues.

Types of Variation

Figures 2-1 through 2-3 present three multi-vari charts that illustrate common types of variation that can occur in the product: within-piece variation, piece-to-piece variation, and time-to-time variation. (Other types of variation, such as side-to-side, operator-to-operator, machine-to-machine, cycle-to-cycle, day-to-day, etc., exist in industry but will not be discussed in this chapter.) The figures are derived from hypothetical operating processes that are making mostly good product. For the purposes of these three figures, assume that measurements were made at two places on the same feature of each piece (as shown in Figure 2-4), and the sampling of pieces was done in groups of five.

   • Figure 2-1 shows significant within-piece variation—measurements made at two different places on the same feature of the same piece vary as much as seven "points" (2 to 9 on piece number 4; this variation is highlighted by a double dotted line). There is little piece-to-piece variation—only pieces 36 and 73 show as much as a 1 "point" difference from the average of the other pieces. The time-to-time variation—from one group of five pieces to the next, each group produced at a different time—is also insignificant. This pattern suggests that whatever process variable is causing the variation is causing it within the piece. Suppose that Figure 2-1 reflects a machining process that was used to make a cylindrical part such as automobile engine piston pins. Excessive within-piece vari-

Figure 2-1. Within-Piece Variation.

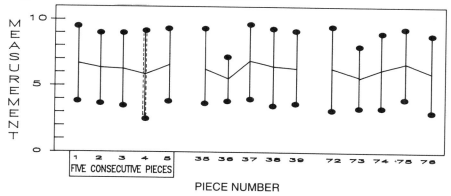

Figure 2-2. Piece-to-Piece Variation.

Figure 2-3. Time-to-Time Variation.

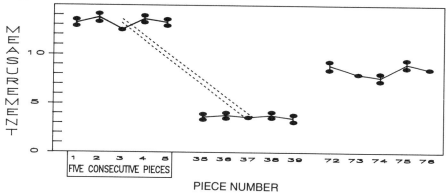

Figure 2-4. Examples of Two Measurements Made on the Same Feature of the Same Piece.

ation would indicate that individual pin diameters are not consistent from one end of the pin to the other.

• Figure 2-2 shows significant piece-to-piece variation (highlighted by a double dotted line). The piece-to-piece variation is as much as 5 "points" (piece number 2 to piece number 3). Within-piece variation, however, is slight—about 1 to 2 "points" on all pieces. Likewise, the variation from time to time is small; that is, the average of the measurements of the first group of five pieces is similar to the averages of the second and third group, even though the samples were taken at different times. This pattern indicates that the variation is caused by one or more process variables that vary excessively from piece to piece.

• Figure 2-3 shows major time-to-time variation, ranging on the measurement scale from about 13 for the first group of five pieces to 4 for the second group (the double dotted line used to highlight the time-to-time variation extends from the average of the first group of pieces to the average of the second group of pieces). The within-piece variation is small—most pieces vary less than 1 "point" (pieces 3, 37, 73, and 76 have no measurable within-piece variation and are therefore plotted as a single point). The piece-to-piece variation is also slight. Thus, the major variation seems to be caused by process variables that vary excessively over time.

The next step after the initial multi-vari analysis would be to determine which variables fit the clues.

Using the Clues

Using the multi-vari technique to identify the process variables that are most likely to be causing product problems may be compared to playing the game of Twenty Questions. This game starts with one person thinking of some physical thing. Another person then has 20 questions to determine what that thing is. The first question is whether the item is animal, vegetable, or mineral. If the answer is animal, two-thirds of the "universe" has been ruled out. The questioner then asks a further narrowing question such as: Does it have four legs? If the answer is yes, humans, birds, fish, and insects are ruled out, and the search is confined to a four-legged animal. The next question would not be whether it is a kangaroo, giraffe, or panda, but rather a narrowing question such as: Is it bigger than a dog? If it is not bigger than a dog, the search is further restricted to a small, four-legged animal. The game continues with questions asked that further reduce the field of possible answers.

Both Twenty Questions and key variable isolation using multi-vari work in this narrowing fashion. This approach contrasts sharply with the method of continuing to guess randomly at the answer. The continued guessing method might be compared to learning in Twenty Questions that the item had been narrowed down to a four-legged animal, smaller than a dog and then guessing chrysanthemum. The answer, however, cannot be chrysanthemum because it does not fit the clues. Using the multi-vari technique, the investigator can set aside the investigation of those process variables that are not likely to be causing problems and concentrate on those that are most likely to be key variables.

Multi-Vari vs. Designed Experiments

It is important here to understand the difference between the multi-vari technique and the technique known as designed experiments, another method of locating the key variable(s). In a multi-vari study, the manufacturing process is intentionally not disturbed. A stratified sample is selected from an ongoing process to represent what happens during regular production without interrupting that process; that is, products manufactured during a multi-vari study are the same as products made when a study is not being run.

In a designed experiment, on the other hand, an investigator creates a special experiment in which process input variables are intentionally adjusted either individually or in combinations in order to determine which variables may be causing the problem. Multi-vari studies may be used on their own or in conjunction with designed experiments. For example, through a multi-vari study, an investigator may narrow down to three the process variables suspected of causing product problems. The investigator then might design a specific type of experiment to test the three variables and determine which of the three is the key variable.

Chapter 3

Quantification: The Initial Diagnostic Step

Many manufacturing problems go unsolved for long periods of time because investigators have not quantified the product characteristic that is being investigated. Product characteristics such as physical dimensions, electrical resistance, voltage, and weight are by their nature quantifiable. Product problems may also involve defects in characteristics that are visual, pertaining to workmanship, or cosmetic rather than dimensional in nature. Visual, workmanship, and cosmetic characteristics are designated as *attributes* and are typically rated only "good" or "bad," "acceptable" or "unacceptable," "satisfactory" or "unsatisfactory." These attribute ratings, however, are not sensitive enough for problem-solving efforts. When a problem-solving effort involves the evaluation of attributes the industrial investigator must first develop a numerical scale for measuring them. As Lord Kelvin, the British mathematician and physicist, advised more than 100 years ago: "When you can measure what you're speaking about and express it in numbers, you know something about it, but when you cannot measure it, when you cannot express it in numbers, your knowledge is of a meager and unsatisfactory kind." Even today many companies have not learned that lesson well enough. Lord Kelvin's advice means that, "You can't make what you can't measure because you don't know when you've got it made."

Quantifying Attributes

The following example illustrates the importance of quantifying visual or physical defects. The engineers of a company were having trouble with a particular defect while producing a laminated plastic product. They would run a number of units one way and count the percent defective, then run a number of units another way and count that percent defective. Percent defective calculations, however, do not consider the degree of defectiveness. After struggling with the process improvement project the problem-solving team replaced the percent defective method with a numerical rating scale shown in Figure 3-1. This scale uses numbers 0 to 5 to evaluate the product. Note that nothing in this numerical scale states whether the product is acceptable. The scale simply provides a rating that can be used for determining changes in the manufacturing process. The objective of creating such a scale was to solve the defect problem, not to decide whether to ship the product.

Companies may, however, devise other formats that combine attribute rating scales with product acceptability information. Figure 3-2 is an example of such a scale. The scale starts at 0, which is perfect, and goes up to 8, which denotes a very severe defect. These numerical ratings are used during process improvement projects. The left-hand column of Figure 3-2 denotes product acceptability levels. A company might be able to ship product rated 0 to 4 (ship on "green" or "yellow")

Figure 3-1. Numerical Rating Scale.

```
0 — PERFECT.
1 — VERY FAINT—INCIPIENT, USUALLY NEAR A CORNER.
2 — DEFINITELY SHOWING—BUT LESS THAN THE AVERAGE SEEN DUR-
    ING AN EPIDEMIC.
3 — AVERAGE—SEEN WHEN DEFECTS ARE OCCURING, USUALLY
    GOING ACROSS FULL BOARD—MODERATELY SEVERE.
4 — HEAVY INVOLVEMENT—TYPICALLY GOING ACROSS FULL BOARD,
    BLOTCHY, BUT NOT A SOLID MASS.
5 — AS BAD AS IT EVER GETS—TOTAL INVOLVEMENT.
```

Figure 3-2. Numerical Rating Scale with Acceptance Guide.

GREEN	0	PERFECT
GREEN	1	NEARLY PERFECT
GREEN	2	TOP COMMERCIAL
YELLOW	3	GOOD COMMERCIAL
YELLOW	4	FAIR COMMERCIAL
RED	5	POOR COMMERCIAL
RED	6	MAJOR DEFECT
RED	7	SEVERE DEFECT
RED	8	VERY SEVERE DEFECT

to some customers, while other customers might accept only product rated 0 to 2 (ship on "green" only). In Figure 3-2, a "red" identification means the product is not acceptable for shipment to any customer.

A numerical rating scale such as that shown in Figure 3-2 provides consistent quantification so that a company will not make the mistake of shipping an unacceptable product and perhaps lose a customer. Such a scale creates a visual gauge so that all inspectors evaluate the product in the same way. The numerical score reflects the overall appearance of the product, rather than individual defects of the product; the size, combination, pattern, and placement of defects are all important factors in determining the score. However, because there will always be a certain amount of subjectivity in viewing the product, the score will also be somewhat subjective. Therefore, each attribute rating system should be backed up by prominently displayed visual samples of each defect level.

Panel of Experts

To develop scales such as those shown in Figure 3-1 and 3-2, usually a panel of experts is assembled to look at samples of the product and come to a consensus. A consensus means that all persons involved agree on the figures, which then become the standard. On many of the samples the experts will agree on the score. However, there are usually some samples about which there is a disagreement. After assigning scores to those samples on which there is agreement, the panel returns to those about which there were disagreements and reviews them until agreement is reached. Once the scale has been established, other people who will be judging the product—such as the foreman, the general foreman, and the operators—are brought in and their vision is calibrated.

An example of how a panel might work toward consensus follows.

> An investigator was working on a visual standard program involving 11 panel members who included operators, inspectors, manufacturing supervisors, and quality control personnel. The panel had finally obtained agreement on all but one sample. One inspector insisted the sample was a 3, while most of the others said it was a 2. A few panel members began by insisting the sample was a 3 but were convinced during the discussion that it was a 2. The inspector remained firm that it was a 3. In exasperation, the superintendent pointed at him and blurted, "You are overruled." The investigator quickly countered that there was no overruling in consensus programs. Finally, a quality engineer suggested that the product be buffed for a better look. One of the operators brought the product out to the shop floor, buffed it, and returned to the panel. The buffing highlighted the defects, and when everyone examined the product again, they all agreed that the sample was a 3. At times, *refining* needs to be done to the sample before all agree, but this is what is involved in a consensus decision.
>
> In addition, vision needs to be *recalibrated* periodically because visual impressions are always subjective

and may shift over time. Some inspectors become less careful and their scores get looser, while others become more careful, even nitpicking. Certain inspectors may even reach the point where they feel they should reject anything made in the plant. Also, during the last two or three days of the month inspectors' vision may change drastically, as they face the end-of-the-month schedule. A formal quantification system and periodic review of that system or recalibration with inspectors reduces or eliminates these inconsistencies.

Chapter 4

The Case of Out-of-Specification Coil Resistance

The following case history describes how a multi-vari study solved a longstanding problem at a company where transformers were a major product. The company had been consistently scrapping about 4% of the transformers it made, which were out of specification for coil resistance. Coil resistance is an indicator of length of the wire and thereby the number of turns on the coil. The number of turns on the coil determines electrical characteristics of the transformers.

The company made transformer coils on a 12-headed coil-winding machine. After the coils were wound they were sent through a series of processes in order to make transformers and finally the coil resistance was measured. The chief engineer of the company asked an industrial investigator to determine the cause of the problem. During the initial discussion the engineer offered some ideas such as, "The power company has voltage surges that affect this operation." He also stated that, "At the end of the day, when we run second shift, the power changes from mostly industrial and commercial to mostly residential." After the chief engineer had described these and other process input variables, all of which were electrical, the investigator decided to start the investigation by running a multi-vari study.

To begin the study the quality control manager and the investigator collected five consecutive coils, at each of three times during one day, from each of the 12 winding heads, and brought the coils directly to the resistance-measuring equipment.

Evaluating the Data

Figure 4-1 shows coil resistances from 3 of the 12 heads (numbers 4, 7, and 8). A small percentage of the coils was above specification and the multi-vari study clearly shows that the problem was an incorrectly adjusted head. Head number 8 was set too close to the high limit; the coil resistances were not centered on the nominal (target) value. Many of the coils from head number 8 were within specification, but some (identified by squares in Figure 4-1) were over the limit. On any given head, the coil-to-coil variation was small. The time-to-time variation was also negligible and there was essentially no change between the first and second shift. After analyzing the multi-vari study, the investigator decided that the corrective action should be to adjust head number 8 so that the coil resistances

Figure 4-1. Coil Resistance Data in Multi-Vari Format.

were centered on the target value, routinely draw a sample from each head, and, if necessary, readjust the process (the individual head) so that the coil resistances were centered on the nominal value.

Additional Benefits

The multi-vari study had an additional result besides correction of the problem. The study showed that variation from one coil to another (on the same head) and from time-to-time was very small, which meant that once the heads were set correctly and monitored periodically there would be even less variation than the specification allowed. Thus, the company could build to a tighter specification than had existed. The company then had the opportunity of charging a higher price for a premium product and/or trying to reach a select segment of the market. In this situation, the solution to the problem meant more than 100% good product; it meant a potentially new market for the company.

The important point to recognize in this case is that the product was used to lead the investigator to the solution. The multi-vari results quickly revealed what was not causing the problem, and that knowledge narrowed the field of investigation. The problem was not solved by the traditional engineering approach of trying to guess the answer. The chief engineer had tried this approach—had, in effect, tried to "tell" the process what was wrong. The engineer thought that the problem was electrical when actually it was mechanical. Using multi-vari studies, investigators let the process do the talking and then listened to the process.

The Case of Out-of Specification Coil Resistance

Step 1—Provide focus. This chronic quality problem caused the greatest number of transformer rejections.

Step 2—Get close to the problem. After an initial discussion the investigator and quality control manager entered the factory and observed the coil-winding process.

Step 3—Quantify the output. The existing regular method of measuring coil resistance made this step straightforward.

Step 4—Run multi-vari study(ies). The multi-vari study provided the key for solving the problem by revealing that one head was set off target. Initial guesses had focused on electrical factors while the actual problem resulted from a mechanical factor.

Step 5—Design experiment(s). Success of the multi-vari study eliminated the need for this step.

Step 6—Turn the problem on and off. The investigator turned the problem on and off by adjusting the settings of the heads.

Step 7—Optimize. An ability to change the results at will obviated the need for optimization studies.

Step 8—Install process controls on key variable(s). Resistance measurements of periodic samples from each head guided the necessary adjustments of the heads. The heads tended to be very stable so this process control was simple and effective.

Step 9—Measure before and after results. Before the study about 4% of the transformers had been defective, whereas after the study 0% were defective. Furthermore, the total variation was now so much less than the tolerance that it presented the company with an opportunity to charge more for its premium product and/or reach a select segment of the market.

Chapter 5

Interactions

The cause of a manufacturing problem is often more complex than one or two key variables acting independently. Sometimes two or more process variables act together to produce a result different from that of either (or both) variables acting alone. This combined result is called an **interaction**. An everyday example of an interaction is what happens when sodium and chlorine combine to make sodium chloride or table salt. Either sodium or chlorine by itself acts as a deadly poison if swallowed. When sodium and chlorine interact, however, they produce table salt—a "result" very much different from either sodium or chlorine acting alone.

Figure 5-1 shows a typical interaction between two industrial process variables—temperature and pressure. A scenario involving these variables might be as follows:

> An engineer is concerned about the effect of the two variables in one of the company's processes when they are at their high and low limits. He decides to run a test, holding everything constant except the one variable being tested. Therefore, he performs his first test holding temperature constant at the high level while he sets the pressure at the low level. He gets a result of 5. Then he raises the pressure to the high level and gets a result of 11. The engineer returns to his office and writes in his logbook, "When I raise the pressure from the low level to the high level the output goes up." A valid conclusion.
>
> The next day the engineer decides to verify his results. He returns to the shop floor and again holds the temperature constant, but this time at the low level. He adjusts the pressure to the low level and gets a result of

Figure 5-1. Two Ways of Showing the Results of Tests Involving Interactions.

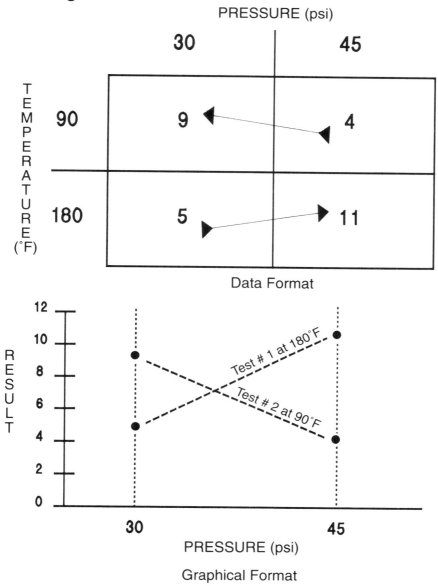

Data Format

Graphical Format

9. Then he adjusts the pressure to the high level and gets a result of 4. This time the engineer notes in his logbook: "As I raise the pressure from the low level to the high level the output goes down. Yesterday it went up. I know what the problem is—poor supervision and apathetic operators."

The cause of the problem, however, is not poor supervision and apathetic operators. The cause of the problem is an interaction between temperature and pressure. Interactions are common in manufacturing processes.

To describe an interaction, the word *depends* must be used. In the previous example, to describe the effect of adjusting the pressure one must say, "The result depends on the temperature at which the test is run." Or, to describe the effect of adjusting the temperature one must say, "The result depends on the pressure at which the test is run." Since the engineer is unaware of the effects of interactions, he may not find them by running tests in which only one process variable is adjusted or changed while everything else is held constant. Other testing methods may be required to detect the effects of interaction.

While multi-vari analysis is usually the first choice in key variable isolation, interactions can confuse the results because multi-vari testing is intentionally performed without correcting or adjusting process input variables. To identify interactions, process variables must intentionally be adjusted in appropriate combinations and sequences. There are a number of techniques that can be used to evaluate interactions; of these, designed experiments probably have the longest history of use in industry.

Chapter 6

The Case of the Flat Beer

By John M. Reddy

When most of the breweries decided to switch to aluminum cans, they experienced a new quality problem unique to aluminum—leaks that seemed to be caused by small pieces of aluminum oxide called "stringers" at the rim of the cans. Cans without oxide stringers did not leak. While no spillage of liquid occurred, the carbon dioxide in the beer would occasionally escape, and in some rare instances the customer received a can of flat beer. Since the incidence of flat beer was only 60 per million cans, or 0.006%, virtually all breweries accepted this apparently trivial quality problem. Most executives in the brewing industry at that time decided that the cost savings realized by the use of aluminum more than compensated for the slight deterioration in quality. The cost/quality trade-off reasoning, however, was not acceptable to one brewer. This company insisted on high quality throughout the entire process. Knowingly sending out a defective product was inconsistent with company policies and could not be tolerated. The company, therefore, decided to assemble a problem-solving team in order to determine the cause of the problem.

Planning the Problem-Solving Approach

A designed experiment to evaluate a problem level as small as 60 parts per million would have been too large and unwieldy to be practical. Thus, the problem-solving team decided to use an approach that involved forcing or aggravating manufacturing conditions in order to obtain data that would highlight variation from one operating condition to another. To accomplish this goal, the team obtained a large sample of cans with stringers to feed into the stations where the cans were filled and sealed. A month of searching by dozens of people in the company's can-making department provided the team with 240 examples of oxide stringers in the rim area of unfilled cans.

While the actual cost of the search for these cans was small, the psychological benefits of including many people in the problem-solving process were great. Excitement built as the word passed through the company that the problem-solving team was coming to grips with a stubborn process problem. Difficult steps can often produce positive results as they did in this case: the actual cost was slight but many people gained a sense of accomplishment in attacking a supposedly impossible problem.

Setting Up the Experiment

Quantification is a prerequisite for this type of study, and the team used the straightforward approach of dividing the 240 cans into three grades of 80 each. In grade 1 the oxide stringers were about $1/64$ inch long; in grade 2, they ranged around $1/32$ inch; and in grade 3 they were about $1/16$ inch long. Piece-to-piece identification was achieved by placing one colored, indelible dot on the can just below the stringer for grade 1, two dots for grade 2, and three dots for grade 3. By placing the dots in this way, the team could tell the exact location of the stringer during the entire process. In several cases the location of the stringer provided important clues for identifying the key variables.

The team then turned its attention to the filling/sealing process. Each of the four filling/sealing stations consisted of 24 separate heads. This is analogous to 24 different "machines" ganged together on one base. Since each head was a unique "machine," the team agreed that it had to know which head filled and sealed which can. The normal production records showed leakage rates* for each station but not for each head. Control charts indicated that some stations at times produced more defects than other stations. However, there seemed to be no way to identify which head within each station produced what percentage of defective product. For the experiment, the team found a way to make a small mark on each can going through head number 1. Identifying the cans filled by a specific head could then be done easily because the cans were fed into a conveyor in which the order of filling and sealing was strictly maintained.

The team judged that measuring head-to-head variation rather than only station-to-station variation[†] would probably yield more information because past production records showed that the station-to-station variation was not great enough to identify the cause of the problem over the long term. The underlying principle in this decision was that problem solving usually involves delving into areas where the largest differences can be found. Because overall there was so little difference between the stations, one station was arbitrarily chosen for the test.

One final step of planning proved to be necessary. The team had available 240 cans with stringers, or 10 cans for each of the 24 heads. Team members believed they could tell a good can from a bad one. But was that the way the process would see it? In other words, could the team be assured that so-called good cans would actually be defect-free? These questions prompted the team to decide to collect 960 good cans, a relatively easy step because so few cans had oxide stringers in the

---

*The leakage rates for each of the four stations in the normal production records were determined as follows: As a routine test, individual filled and sealed cans were randomly selected from each station and placed in a test device. This device was able to detect and measure the rate at which carbon dioxide escaped from the can. The rate was measured in parts per million of carbon dioxide per unit of time. When the rate of leakage exceeded a specified limit, the can was considered defective, that is, that product item was defective. If the rate of carbon dioxide leakage were very high, enough carbon dioxide could escape to result in a "flat" can of beer by the time a consumer attempted to consume it.

†Station-to-station variation was determined by comparing the percentage of cans from each station that exceeded the maximum leakage rate specification.

rim area. Thus, the team had available 40 "good" cans and 10 cans with stringers for each of the 24 filling/sealing heads.

This type of careful planning is a mark of good problem solvers. The planning and preparation for the experiment took more than a month. Collecting and marking samples, modifying the equipment to indicate which head filled and sealed which can, and obtaining permission from company management all required considerable time and effort. Such planning ensures that when a problem-solving team completes an experiment, it has confidence in the results. Industrial experiments also require careful coordination with company management. Production facilities are put in place to produce salable product, not to run experiments. Thus, another characteristic of competent industrial problem solvers is that they respect production management's responsibilities and are willing to spend time to assure that running the experiment is practical and does not unnecessarily disturb production requirements.

Running the Experiment

The team could have decided to run the "good" cans first followed by the "bad" ones, the worst possible decision. Reversing this order has no more merit. Running an experiment in clusters of good followed by bad or the reverse supposes that the process will stay absolutely constant during the course of the experiment—probably an erroneous assumption. Some members of the team were willing to follow a simple rotation scheme of four "good" cans and one "bad" can. As it turned out, this method would have worked. But there is always the possibility that any cyclical scheme will coincide with cyclical variations in the process. Considering all the work that had gone into the experiment, it would have been unwise to take this chance when a risk-free method was readily at hand. The best approach in such cases is to mix the bad product and good product together randomly. By random mixing, the results cannot erroneously be confounded or mixed up with cyclical patterns in the process itself.

During the experiment, none of the 960 "good" cans proved to be leakers* while 93 of the 240 cans with stringers leaked. Some filling/sealing heads (numbers 1 and 4) were fed 10 cans with stringers and produced no leakers. Head number 24 had 10 out of 10 leakers. The others had defect rates between zero and 10. The cause of the leaking cans was determined to be an interaction between two key variables—filling/sealing heads that were marginally adjusted and cans that had stringers at the rim.

Whenever a can was found to be a leaker, the leak always occurred at the point of the oxide stringer. Investigation also determined that filling/sealing heads that had zero leakers out of 10 cans with stringers and those heads that produced 10 leakers out of 10 cans with stringers had filled and sealed cans with all three grades of stringers. The size of the stringer was not a factor in whether a can leaked. In retrospect, the team realized that it did not need to measure and identify the size of the stringer, only note its presence. If the size of the stringer had been important, however, but had not been recorded, a major portion of the clues to the problem would have been lost and there would have been no practical way to reconstruct the results. It is always better to get somewhat more detail at the beginning of an investigation than too little.

Correcting the Problem

The team next performed a thorough investigation comparing spring tensions, dimensions, flatness, squareness, edge smoothness, geometry, and so forth, between the filling/sealing heads that produced no leakers out of 10 cans with oxide stringers and those heads that produced 10 leakers out of 10 cans with oxide stringers.

Once these measurements were taken, the team determined the correct specifications from those heads that could

*As noted earlier in this chapter, *leak* or *leaker* refers to the fact that the escape of carbon dioxide from the can exceeded allowable rates. There was never leakage of beer.

make nonleaking cans even with aluminum that contained oxide stringers in the critical rim area.

One essential step remained—a quality audit under production conditions. After the filling/sealing heads were adjusted to the specifications derived from the best performers, the team observed an entire day's production of several million cans. The result: not a single leaking can. In the past there would have been as many as 200. A second day's test with no reported leaks confirmed that the team had indeed discovered the key variables and had derived the correct specifications.

Conclusion

It is important to emphasize that the correct specifications came from the process itself—not from the engineers. This approach is based on *consulting with the process* to determine those conditions that will always produce good product. However, while this experiment was technically interesting and even innovative, an important lesson was that management determines the quality level. The management of the company had considered any defective product unacceptable. The problem-solving team, knowing management's position, solved a seemingly impossible problem at a cost that was small compared to the potential deterioration of the company's quality reputation.

The Case of the Flat Beer

Step 1—Provide focus. Management decided that the incidence of flat beer of 60 cans per million was unacceptable.

Step 2—Get close to the problem. The problem-solving team looked closely at the four beer-filling/sealing stations each with 24 filling heads.

Step 3—Quantify the output. The team quantified the size of the oxide stringers so they could be kept separate during the experiment and related to the degree of leakage.

Step 4—Run multi-vari study(ies). Existing data showed that the four filling/sealing stations had similar leakage rates so one filling/sealing station was chosen for the designed experiment. A multi-vari study was not needed.

Step 5—Design experiment(s). The designed experiment variables chosen were four levels of oxide stringers including no oxide stringers and the other variable was the 24 filling/sealing heads on one of the filling stations.

Step 6—Turn the problem on and off. The problem could be turned on and off by varying the conditions of the filling/sealing head key variables.

Step 7—Optimize. The key variables and their interaction were completely defined so an optimizing step was not required.

Step 8—Install process controls on key variable(s). The specifications for the key filling/sealing head variables were corrected so process controls were not needed.

Step 9—Measure before and after results. Before the study there were approximately 60 cans of potentially flat beer produced per million. After the study there were no cans of potentially flat beer produced.

Chapter 7

Designed Experiments

It is not unusual for a large number of process variables to be eliminated as possible key variables during multi-vari analysis. But even if only two or three process variables remain under consideration, determining which of them—or their interactions—are the cause of process problems can present real difficulties. In these cases, multi-vari followed by a designed experiment usually provides the most direct solution.

All properly conducted designed experiments contain four key elements:

1. For practical analysis they must be balanced.

2. To be valid they must be randomized.

3. To give a good estimate of repeatability, more than one replication (more than one test at each set of conditions) should be conducted.

4. A numerical system for measuring attributes and/or dimensions is required. The use of satisfactory or unsatisfactory attribute notation is not sensitive enough and is a major reason that many industrial problems remain unsolved. An agreed-upon numerical system for measuring attributes is necessary. Dimensional measurements usually have agreed-upon numerical systems such as ohms, inches, or pounds, but in some situations numerical systems must be developed.

Figure 7-1 shows a balanced designed experiment with four variables each at two levels, in which there are 16 (2^4) test combinations to be run. In this figure, A, B, C, and D represent process variables such as temperature, pressure, time, and so forth. $A+$, $B-$, and so forth represent the high or low

Figure 7-1. Designed Experiment Layout Grid.

		A−		A+	
		B−	B+	B−	B+
C−	D−				
	D+				
C+	D−				
	D+				

test conditions for the variable. The open squares represent numbers that reflect the results of a particular test: for example, the upper left-hand box represents the results of testing at conditions A −, B −, C −, and D −.

Figure 7-2 compares the results of conventional testing with statistically designed experiments. In conventional testing, investigators attempt to gain information about variables A, B, C, and D, one at a time. A statistically designed experiment, such as that shown in Figure 7-1, provides information about A, B, C, and D, and also determines if there are any two-factor and three-factor interactions. If a second replicate* is run, then the four-factor effects free of residual error can be estimated.

The concept of *residual error* is another important element in understanding designed experiments. The amount of residual error in a designed experiment indicates whether the test design included the correct variable(s). If there is a high resid-

---

*A second replicate refers to rerunning all combinations a second time.

Figure 7-2. Comparison of the Amount of Test Information Provided by Conventional Testing and by a Designed Experiment.

Conventional Testing	Designed Experiment
1. A	1. A
2. B	2. B
3. C	3. C
4. D	4. D
	5. A X B
	6. A X C
	7. A X D
	8. B X C
	9. B X D
	10. C X D
	11. A X B X C
	12. A X B X D
	13. B X C X D
	14. A X C X D
	15. A X B X C X D
	16. RESIDUAL ERROR

ual error—that is, a lot of "noise" in the experiment—the results are saying that something else besides the variables being evaluated is causing the excessive variation, such as lack of repeatability of the test and all other inconsistencies, such as minor fluctuations in the running of the tests. Therefore, the experiment itself tells the investigators how well it was designed and run. This is important because designed experiments can be run with the wrong variables—usually the result of "guessing" the cause of the problem. While these guesses can be helpful in eliminating some variables, the purpose of a designed experiment is to see how much the variables being tested contribute to the variation or if untested variables contribute greatly. In other words, in a designed experiment, the investigator can determine whether the *signal*—the selected variable(s)—stands out above the *noise*—the variables not tested.

The concept of separating the effect of the variables being

tested from the residual error can be difficult to understand. Many people have trouble understanding how investigators can analyze test results to tell which variables and/or interactions are real (significant) and which ones have little or no effect on the results. The following example illustrates how real effects can be separated from residual error or noise.

Figure 7-3. Component Printing Defect Scores Before Cleaning.

A company was using an eight-station printer to print identifying information on electronic components. In Figure 7-3 a group of 29 components is shown in the rectangle at the center of the figure. The numbers to the right of the rectangle indicate the print head (1–8) on which each component was printed. The degree of

Figure 7-4. Component Printing Defect Scores After Cleaning.

printing defectiveness is shown by the numbers to the left of the rectangle; the defect score runs from 0 (no defect) to 4 (maximum defect). Of the 29 components, 12 show some degree of printing defect. In an attempt to eliminate the defects, the company ultrasonically cleaned the 29 components in Freon. Figure 7-4 shows the components after the cleaning. The cleaning had physically removed the residual error—that is, eight of the small printing defects—so that the real culprit, head number 7, stands out as the source of the problem. In Figure 7-3, the real effect, at head number 7, was partially masked by small defects caused by the noise from other heads. When company personnel had looked at Figure 7-3 they did not realize that they were seeing a combination of real effect and residual error.

In the same way, the statistical analysis of a designed experiment separates—mathematically—the significant variables from random noise and places confidence limits on the results of the experiment. Designed experiments are used, in part, to accomplish mathematically what in the electronic component printing example was accomplished physically.

Chapter 8

The Case of Porous Decorative Rings

A company was experiencing an increased level of porosity in the cast decorative rings that it manufactured. Production requirements had increased, and the company was having trouble meeting the demand because scrap rates were too high. A high scrap rate had always existed, but it had not been considered serious because defective rings were returned to the molten metal and remelted. However, with the increased production requirements the company could not afford the extra time to recast many rings. The foreman who had supervised the area for many years and had recently retired had been brought back as a consultant. To find the solution to the problem he experimented with process variables such as pouring rate, pouring height, and the temperature of the molten metal. One of the two suppliers of metal had been notified that the composition of raw material had apparently changed and not to ship any more metal. The consultant foreman had tried every modification he knew and was concerned that he would have to resort to the "old timer's" remedy: when all else fails, throw a cold, raw, unpeeled potato into the molten metal. To help resolve the problem, company management brought in a problem-solving team. When the team arrived in the casting area, the inspectors were rejecting most of the rings for excess porosity and these rings were being remelted.

Quantification

The team determined that the first step in its problem-solving strategy should be quantification. The team collected samples of rings that showed varying degrees of porosity and developed the following numerical rating scale:

1—Very Small Defect
2—Obvious Defect
3—Large Defect
4—Very Large Defect
5—Huge Hole

It was decided that each defect would be rated and a tally kept of the defect scores. In addition, the location of the defect would be plotted in red on a picture of the ring. This type of diagram is known as a **measles chart**.

After developing the rating scale and pictorial representation, the team conducted a multi-vari study. During the study, the team gathered samples of rings in order to determine patterns of variation. The following types of variation were examined: within-ring, ring-to-ring, and time-to-time. It is extremely important to look at within-piece (within-ring) variation whenever possible. In this case, it was necessary to identify the location and size of individual defects. Too often, insufficient information is gathered on within-piece variation and important clues are lost.

Test Results

Figure 8-1 shows the measles chart. The numbers within the ring are the average total defect scores for the entire multi-vari study. These numbers were derived by multiplying the occurrence of a defect on each ring by its defect score. For example, a ring might have one defect with a score of 5, one defect with a score of 4, and one defect with a score of 3. The defect score for this ring would therefore be 12. Six occurrences of defects each with a score of 2 would also result in a score of 12. An average of all the rings is shown in Figure 8-1 because the team found there was so little variation from ring to ring and time to time that an average of all the rings was representative. The largest variation was within the ring.

Figure 8-1. Measles Chart for Ring Defects.

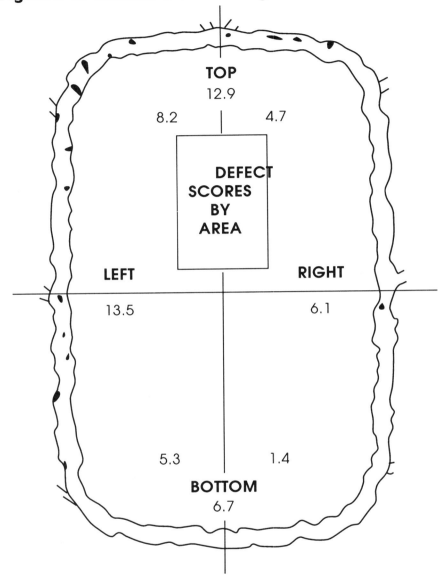

For the entire study the average defect score per ring was 19.6, and the numbers shown within the ring in Figure 8-1 reflect average defect scores for each area. For example, the number 12.9 reflects the average defect score for the top half of the ring, that is, the part of the ring above the horizontal line. The number 6.7 reflects the average defect score for the bottom half of the ring, that is, below the horizontal line. The sum of the top half and bottom half scores (12.9 + 6.7) is 19.6. The number 6.1 reflects the average score for the right-hand half of the ring, that is, the part of the ring to the right of the vertical line. Scores for the right- and left-hand halves of the ring (13.5 + 6.1) also total 19.6. In the same way, each of the four quadrants are scored: for example, the upper right-hand quadrant has a score of 4.7. The total average score for the four quadrants (8.2 + 4.7 + 5.3 + 1.4) also totals 19.6.

The left side of the ring has about twice the average total defect score that the right side has (13.5 versus 6.1) and the top of the ring has about twice the defect score that the bottom of the ring has (12.9 versus 6.7).

If the upper left-hand quadrant of the ring is compared to the lower right-hand quadrant the ratio is about 6 to 1 (8.2 versus 1.4). The other two opposite quadrants are approximately equal, 5.3 versus 4.7. A closer look at the spots on the measles chart shows that the greatest concentration of defects (porosity) occurred around the upper left-hand corner.

When the pattern of defects was quite clear, a team member pointed out that there seemed to be something unusual about the upper left-hand corner of the casting and asked if anyone had any ideas. The foreman said, "Yes, that is where the fan is." When questioned about the fan, the foreman reminded the team that working over molten metal is very hot work and a fan must be used to cool off the operator. Also, with a fan in place the rings can be taken out of the mold sooner because they solidify more quickly. The team also asked if the operator ever used more than one fan or no fan at all. The foreman stated that operators could not work without fans for very long, and in the summer another fan directly in front of the operator was often used.

The Designed Experiment

In many cases, the multi-vari study itself does not solve the problem, but it rules out variables that do not fit and suggests the type of variables that do fit the clues. In this case, the fact that the defects were concentrated in one area reduced the likelihood that the problem was caused by variables such as the supplier of the raw material. The pattern of variation on the measles chart strongly suggested that something was different in the upper left area, and the fan was the most likely suspect. The team then designed an experiment to investigate the effect of the fan on the porosity. The team decided to conduct the experiment in groups of five rings in a row under four different conditions:

1. With the fan in its typical location, near the upper left area of the mold
2. With no fan
3. With the front fan only
4. With both fans

The next step was to use a random number table to select the numbers 1, 2, 3, and 4 to determine the order of using the fans. The foreman explained the test to the operator and assured him that the team would ask him to operate with no fan for only groups of five rings at a time on three occasions. The team chose to run the 20 rings (five in a row at four conditions) three times in order to obtain a different random order each time for the four conditions. By running the experiment three times the team hoped it would be able to "turn the problem on and off."

Figure 8-2 shows the results of the designed experiment in the form of a multi-vari chart. From 8:30 A.M. to 9:30 A.M. the team ran five rings in a row with the left (regular) fan in place, then ran five in a row with no fans, then five in a row with both fans, and finished with five in a row with the front fan only. The team reran the test in a different random order from 10:45 A.M. to 11:45 A.M. During both sets of tests, when only the front fan ran, the defects were significantly less than

Figure 8-2. Decorative Ring Defect Study.

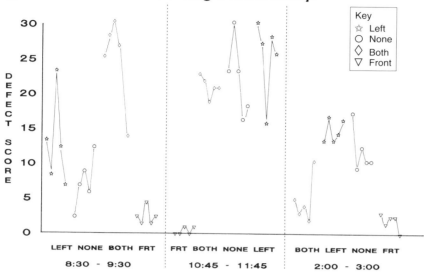

under the other three conditions. The results of the second test run were more dramatic than those of the first run. From 2:00 P.M. to 3:00 P.M. the team ran a third test and again found that the best results occurred when only the front fan was running. The team had let the process do the talking and had listened to it. The process clearly told the team that when only the front fan was used, the defects were drastically reduced. When investigators do not listen to the process they sometimes miss the real causes of problems and use myths to explain them. The idea of throwing a potato into the molten metal is an example of one of these myths.

From production management's perspective, the problem-solving strategy was successful. By using only the front fan the new porosity defect rate was so low that production requirements could easily be met. In fact, the defect rate was so low that essentially all the rings were acceptable. However, 100% inspection was still used to find the few remaining defective rings. In addition to being costly, 100% inspection was not completely effective. It is likely that if production management had the team conduct further investigations the team might have eliminated the porosity or at least reduced it to such an insignificant level that 100% inspection could have been eliminated. The team could have experimented with the front fan by moving it to different heights, angles, distances, speeds, and so forth, as well as trying various size fans.

When the team first looked at the operation it was told that rejections were higher than usual. However, because records were not normally kept it was possible that rejections had not increased but due to higher production requirements the rejections were noticed more. Since the company previously did not have a well-defined numerical scale for determining the degree of porosity, it is also possible that the higher rejection rate simply reflected the increased inspection attention. It is also likely that before the study the difference between accepted and rejected rings was minimal and all rings had too much porosity.

The Case of Porous Decorative Rings

Step 1—Provide focus. Production requirements had increased and the company was having trouble meeting the demand because scrap rates were too high.

Step 2—Get close to the problem. The team entered the casting area, where they found inspectors rejecting most of the rings for excess porosity, and these rings were being remelted.

Step 3—Quantify the output. The team collected samples of rings showing varying degrees of porosity and developed a 0–5 numerical rating scale.

Step 4—Run multi-vari study(ies). The multi-vari study considered within-ring (location on the ring), ring-to-ring for a series of five rings in a row, and time-to-time as potential patterns of variation. The upper left location on the ring stood out as the key pattern of variation. This is where the fan was.

Step 5—Design experiment(s). Having ruled out some of the patterns of variation and focusing on the effect of the fan, the team designed an experiment that included four conditions of fans.

Step 6—Turn the problem on and off. The superior result of the "front fan only" was repeated three times in the experiment. The team had clearly turned the problem on and off.

Step 7—Optimize. The team wanted to optimize the result but manufacturing supervision was pleased and therefore did not want to take the time to pursue the problem to a total solution.

Step 8—Install process controls on key variables. In this problem, with the change made in the manufacturing process, there was no need for control charts.

Step 9—Measure before and after results. Before the study, management was having trouble meeting demand and had a high remelt rate. After the study the problem disappeared.

Chapter 9

The Case of Scrapped Artillery Projectiles

A company that manufactured artillery projectiles was concerned about the potential harm that poor quality could cause and thus called in an industrial investigator to help improve the quality of its product. The company's primary concern lay with the variation in wall thickness, which determined how accurately the projectiles would fly. Rejects from this step in the operation topped the Pareto chart of rejects and cost the company about $100,000 per month.

The manufacturing process started with 5-inch-diameter bars of cold rolled steel sawed to a uniform length each weighing about 26 pounds. This *slug* was put into a machine and formed cold. All units went onto a common conveyor and were then measured by mounting them in a fixture with a dial indicator against the outside wall and a fixed stop against the inside wall. By rotating the projectile, the dial indicator continuously read the wall thickness. The maximum difference allowed between the thickest and thinnest part of the wall was 0.044 inch. The month before the investigator arrived, 10,000 projectiles from the five cold-forming machines had been scrapped because they exceeded the variation limit.

The technical person responsible for the operation stated that the five cold-forming machines were old and temperamental. He suggested that they had personalities of their own, and no one knew what they were going to do next. After discussing the problem with him, the investigator suggested running a multi-vari study. The study began by taking five cold-formed slugs in a row at 9:00 A.M. and 1:00 P.M. (the first shift) and at 4:00 P.M. (the second shift) from each of the five machines. Figure 9-1 shows the results from three of the five machines: the best machine, the worst machine, and the middle machine. The piece-to-piece variation is connected by solid lines and the average time-to-time variation is indicated by dashed lines.

Figure 9-1. Multi-Vari Chart of Projectile Wall Thickness Variations.

As Figure 9-1 indicates, there was very little time-to-time and shift-to-shift variation. In fact, with all the piece-to-piece variation it is surprising that the time-to-time results were as consistent as they were. Because machine-to-machine variation was significant, a best and worst machine could be designated. Time-to-time and shift-to-shift variation, however, were not significant. The piece-to-piece variation on the best machine was relatively small compared to the large piece-to-piece variation on the worst machine. Thus, piece-to-piece variation depended on the machine. When the word *depends* is required to describe an effect, an interaction is present. Interactions cause many of the unsolved problems in industry.

Two clues to the problem were now apparent: there was a difference in the machines, and something was interacting with these machines. Interestingly, four of the lowest readings came from the worst machine. At this point the investigator asked, "What could be interacting with the machines?" One variable that was possibly interacting with the machines was the varying angle of the sawed-off face to the length of the bar. A saw, unlike a milling machine, can act like a serrated knife cutting a watermelon and can cause considerable out-of-squareness.

The Designed Experiment

The investigator used the two clues provided by the multi-vari study to design an experiment of two variables at each of two levels. The two variables selected for the designed experiment were the out-of-squareness of the sawed slugs and the condition of the machines. The two levels of out-of-squareness were the squarest slugs that could be found and the most out-of-square slugs. The two levels of machine condition were the best and worst machines. The squarest and most out-of-square slugs and only the best and worst machines were used because knowledge often lies in the extremes. In this case, the investigator would not have learned more by studying intermediate levels of out-of-squareness or the three machines between the best and worst.

The conditions of the designed experiment were run in a random order to prevent some unknown factor from invalidating the test. When the square slugs were run on the best machine the result was a low amount of wall thickness variation averaging about 0.005 inch and also very consistent results from one slug to the next (see Figure 9-2). When the square slugs were run on the worst machines, the results were again consistent, though at a much higher level—about 0.037 inch. From these data, it was apparent to the investigator that the plungers on the cold-forming machines were misaligned. When the out-of-square slugs were run, variation increased. However, since all square slugs in the worst machine resulted in an average of 0.037 inch variation in wall thickness, the machine must have been, in effect, misaligned 0.037 inch. Similarly, the best machine must have been, in effect, misaligned about 0.005 inch.

The investigator reasoned that as the plunger of the cold-forming machine hit the face of a slug it could either accent the out-of-squareness or compensate for it, depending on the angle at which the plunger hit the face. This would explain why some results from the worst machine could be very good. The misaligned plunger on the machine and the out-of-squareness of the slugs were either canceling or adding to each other. The results confirmed the theory that out-of-square slugs were interacting with the misalignment of the machine. However, there was an interaction beyond the amount of out-of-squareness that related to how the out-of-squareness was oriented to the misalignment.

To confirm this interaction—slug orientation with machine misalignment—the investigator obtained slugs and measured their out-of-squareness and marked which way they were out of square. The investigator then put the slugs into the worst machine in a way that the misalignment and out-of-squareness would add to one another. Next, out-of-square slugs were placed in the worst machine so that the misalignment and out-of-squareness would tend toward canceling each other. Therefore, the results depended on how the misalignment of the machine was oriented to the out-of-squareness of the slug.

Figure 9-2. Designed Experiment Data in Multi-Vari Format.

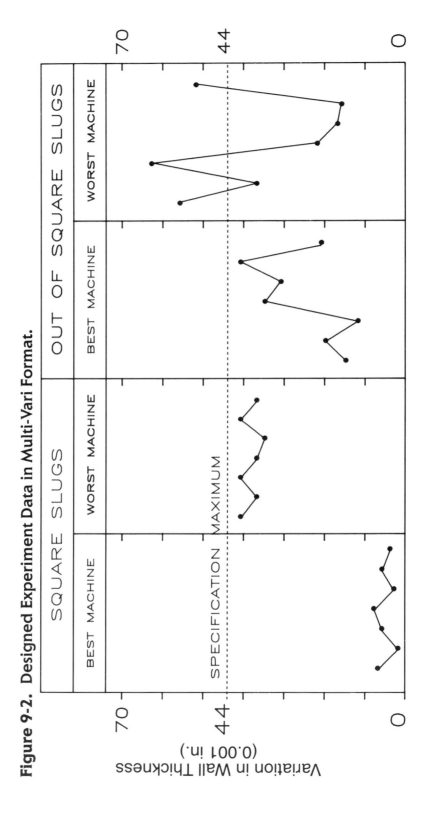

The four key elements described in Chapter 7 were applied to this designed experiment:

1. The experiment was balanced because the same number of projectiles (seven) was used in each of the four combinations.

2. A random number table was used to decide the order in which the test conditions would be run. If the order in which the test conditions were run had not been randomized, some other variable might have changed during the test, and the investigator would not have known it. In Figure 9-2, the results generally became worse moving from left to right. Without randomization the investigator might have suspected that things were getting worse as time went on. By randomly returning to the four conditions, and the results coming back to where they were the last time that condition was tested, the test indicated that the test condition—not some other uncontrolled variable—caused the variation.

3. Seven replicates were tested. Whenever there is a large amount of variation, it is best to test many replicates. The large variation in Figure 9-1 indicated that a number of replicates was required. This was important because some of the best (lowest) readings on the out-of-square slugs on the worst machine were lower than the worst (highest) readings with the out-of-square slugs on the best machine. If only three replicates had been run, and only the lowest three readings of the out-of-square slugs on the worst machine and only the highest three readings of the out-of-square slugs on the best machine had been obtained, the investigator might have erroneously concluded that with out-of-square slugs it was better to use the worst machine. This error would have rendered the test results worse than useless—they would have been misleading.

4. The study already included a system for measuring the thickness of the wall all around the circumference of the projectile. If there had not been a system for measuring this dimension, the investigator would have had to devise one.

Turning the Problem On and Off

Before a manufacturing problem can be considered solved, it must be able to be "turned on and off." In this case, then, the next step was for the investigator to demonstrate that he could turn the problem on and off. The investigator used the worst machine and asked the technical person how he wanted the next projectile to turn out. He said he wanted a very good one. Since the investigator now knew the machine's misalignment, and in which direction it was misaligned, he chose a slug that had a large amount of out-of-squareness and lined it up so that the out-of-squareness of the slug and the misalignment of the machine would tend toward canceling each other. The result was quite good. The technical person thought that the investigator was lucky and asked him to make another projectile— this time a bad one. A slug very much out-of-square was rotated to the opposite direction so that the out-of-squareness and misalignment added to each other. This time the resulting projectile was quite bad. The investigator proceeded in this way until it was agreed that he could predict how a projectile would turn out.

The investigator then used square slugs in each machine to determine the amount and direction of misalignment. The machines were adjusted using square slugs as test samples. The investigator also placed a median chart on the cold-forming machines and on the saw line so squareness could be controlled. The month following these adjustments the number of rejects was 18, compared to 10,000 rejects on a similar production volume at the start of the study. Losses per month fell from $100,000 to $180.

Conclusion

From the results of the multi-vari study and designed experiment it was clear that the problem had two components: the machines were misaligned and the nonsquare slugs were interacting with the misaligned machines. The interaction effect was a mystery to the people operating the machines because sometimes a machine yielded a bad result and sometimes a good result. Because the slugs were out-of-square a widely varying amount, no one knew how much the machines were misaligned. The investigator was able to use square slugs to determine the amount and direction of misalignment and correct each machine. Even if the slugs were out-of-square a small amount, good results could still be obtained.

It had been common practice for the operators to get onto the machines and use a sledgehammer to drive in shims to align the machine. However, with unknown amounts of out-of-squareness and the random orientation of the face of the slug, no one knew exactly how much a machine was misaligned or in which direction. The investigator did not change the method of shimming the machines, but now the operators knew how much to shim and in what direction. The use of square slugs ensured that the proper shims were in place.

As previously mentioned, a manufacturing problem cannot be considered solved until it can be turned on and off. Too frequently in industry when a major problem exists people change a dozen things and the defect level goes down. Then they cross their fingers, walk away, and hope the problem does not return. There are two reasons that people walk away from the problem. First, they do not really know which of the dozen things helped, and they do not want anyone changing anything because the problem might reappear. However, most problems do return because they were not solved—they were temporarily "beaten into submission." A second reason people walk away is because management assigns them to a "hotter fire," rather than allowing them the time to find the real cause, and, ultimately, a solution to prevent the return of the problem. Management usually reasons that, "The fire is out, so why waste time on it?" Unfortunately, this common practice allows the fire to return again and again.

The Case of Scrapped Artillery Projectiles

Step 1—Provide focus. Excess variation in wall thickness topped the Pareto chart for scrap and cost the company tens of thousands of dollars each month.

Step 2 — Get close to the problem. The industrial investigator analyzed the operation and found that workers sawed cold rolled steel to length and then cold formed the steel on one of the five cold-forming machines.

Step 3 — Quantify the output. Inspectors measured the variation in wall thickness by mounting the projectiles in a fixture with a fixed stop against the inside wall and a dial indicator against the outside wall. During the rotating of a projectile the dial indicator continuously read wall thickness.

Step 4 — Run multi-vari study(ies). The investigator ran the multi-vari study considering projectile-to-projectile (piece-to-piece), machine-to-machine for the five comparable machines, time-to-time within the shift, and shift-to-shift.

Step 5 — Design experiment(s). The investigator designed and ran an experiment using the variables suggested by the pattern of variation in the multi-vari studies.

Step 6 — Turn the problem on and off. This essential step proved the reality of the solution to the people responsible for the machines. The investigator made defective or good projectiles at will once the two key variables and their interaction were identified.

Step 7 — Optimize. The ability to vary the results at will eliminated the need for optimization with traditional optimization experiments.

Step 8 — Install process controls on key variable(s). The investigator established a control chart on the two key operations to keep them under control.

Step 9 — Measure before and after results. During the month before the study inspectors had rejected and scrapped 10,000 projectiles at a cost of about $10 each. The number of rejected projectiles fell to 18 in a similar production volume following the institution of recommended adjustments and controls on the process. Losses per month fell from $100,000 to $180.

Chapter 10

The Case of Shorts on Dust Cover Seals

In the following case, quantification of defects helped solve the problem that one company had with a high scrap rate on injection-molded dust cover seals. The operations personnel of the company were convinced that raw material composition was the cause of the problem because there had been a recent change in suppliers.

A number of problems were encountered during the plastic molding operation. These problems included such visual defects as shorts, distortion, blisters, splits, and thick flash. Thick flash was not actually a defect, but it wastes material and therefore is undesirable. The initial diagnostic step was to establish a numerical scale to rate these defects. If the product had no defects, it was rated a 0; a minor defect (but not rejectable) was a 1; a barely rejectable defect was a 2; a major defect was a 3; and a severe defect was a 4.

The investigator who had been called in suggested running a multi-vari study to determine the type of variation, such as within-piece; within-mold (from one cavity to the next); shot-to-shot; heat-to-heat; time-to-time throughout the day; or from one batch of raw material to another. Operations personnel suspected the raw material because they felt they had previously achieved better results.

The investigator decided to record and plot the defect score for "shorts" because it was the largest defect category on the Pareto chart (see Figure 10-1). A data sheet showing the position of the 16 cavities in the mold was drawn so that defect location and severity could be plotted in a technique similar to a measles chart. Figure 10-2 presents that data sheet showing

Figure 10-1. Pareto Chart of Molding Defects.

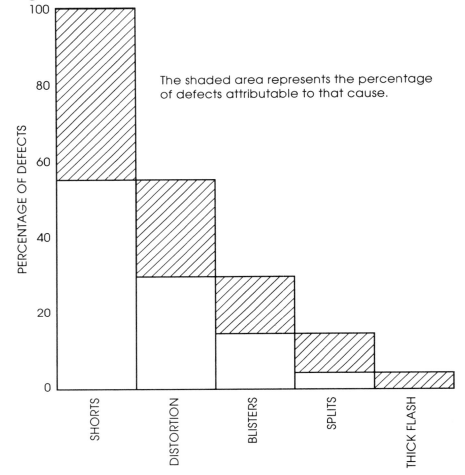

The shaded area represents the percentage of defects attributable to that cause.

results at 10:17 A.M. At that time, the only defects were on the "right-hand" side of the seals, suggesting the occurrence of within-piece variation. In addition, of the 16 cavities, the two defective seals were on the right-hand side of the mold in the center, suggesting there was also within-mold variation.

Figure 10-3 shows a heat that was run at 4:06 P.M. and indicates that the area containing defects had spread out. The investigator decided that the pattern pointed to a possible problem with the way the two halves of the mold fit together, a temperature problem that existed to a different extent at dif-

Figure 10-2. Defect Chart Data Sheet for 10:17 A.M.

ferent times (that is, time-to-time variation), or perhaps an interaction between the two variables.

Using the Clues

The investigator now had several clues: the severity of the problem seemed to vary from time to time, though time-to-time variation might actually be heat-to-heat variation since

Figure 10-3. Defect Chart Data Sheet for 4:06 P.M.

DATA SHEET

DEFECT *Shorts*

DATE *9/17* **TIME** *16:06*

HEAT NO. *11* **MAT'L BATCH NO.** *D0506*

each time was a different heat. The cause of the problem had something to do with location and position because the location of the defect was positional within the cavity and positional within the mold. All of these clues, plus the fact that the same raw material was used for both runs (heats), pointed out that the process variable originally suspected—a change in raw material—was not the cause of the problem. The investigator determined that there were two key variables—excessive variation in the temperature of the injected plastic and an improper fit of the mold halves.

Conclusion

This case demonstrates an important difference between the traditional engineering approach to problem solving and the key variable isolation approach. The traditional approach looks for the causes of product problems by running one day on one raw material, machine setting, or condition, and then running another raw material, machine setting, or condition the next day. But too often with the traditional approach, many factors change between the two runs. With the key variable isolation approach, first a numerical rating scale for visual and physical attributes is developed. Then investigators evaluate the product in much more detail, use a much smaller sample size, and run for a specific, short period of time without changing process conditions. If evaluation of variation over a longer term is required, another small sample can be taken later. The key variable isolation approach provides numerical data that are used to eliminate unimportant variables and focus on the specific variables—the key variable(s)—that are causing the defects in the product.

The Case of Shorts on Dust Cover Seals

Step 1—Provide focus. Shorts was the largest cause for defects on the Pareto chart.

Step 2—Get close to the problem. The investigator and the key technical people reviewed the injection molding process.

Step 3—Quantify the output. The investigator helped the people develop a numerical scale to rate the defects from 0 to 4.

Step 4—Run multi-vari study(ies). The investigator outlined a multi-vari study to look at types of variation such as within-piece, within-mold (cavity-to-cavity), shot-to-shot, heat-to-heat, time-to-time, and batch-to-batch of raw material.

Step 5—Design experiment(s). The team did not run a designed experiment because when the engineer saw the clear pattern on the multi-vari measles chart, he knew what the cause was.

Step 6—Turn the problem on and off. When the indicated corrections were made the problem disappeared and could be partially returned by reintroducing one of the two causes. The temperature could be turned on and off. Of course, once the mold was repaired it was not broken again.

Step 7—Optimize. Optimization was not necessary because the problem was completely eliminated and could be turned back on partially.

Step 8—Install process controls on key variable(s). With a new specification on temperature no new process controls were needed.

Step 9—Measure before and after results. After the two fixes were completed on what had been the top item on the Pareto chart for defects, defects were now nonexistent.

Chapter 11

The Case of Rejects on a Multicavity Compression Molder

A manufacturer of molded plastic components used several multicavity-forming machines for molding tamperproof covers for containers. After they were formed, the covers were dropped into a bucket. A random sample then was taken from the bucket for visual and dimensional inspection. Despite this inspection, some of the company's customers had complained about visual and/or dimensional defects. Because of these complaints, the company assembled a problem-solving team. In this case, the team found that there were two significant problems: excessive dimensional variation and visual defects. After the team studied the process, it investigated the quantification of the visual and dimensional defects. By their very nature, the physical dimensions were already on a numerical scale. However, evaluating the visual defects required the creation of a numerical scale for rating each defect. The team took additional time to prepare this numerical scale before beginning the multi-vari study. Visual defects evaluated included plastic "strings," feathering, flash, bent edges, edges damaged from stripping, and holes (short shots).

The Multi-Vari Study

In its investigation the team viewed each cavity as if it were a separate process. This was an important decision because any cavity might produce units different from another cavity. Before the team was assembled, production personnel had believed that the inspection procedure included the drawing of a random sample from a single process. In fact, relatively few samples were drawn from numerous separate lots or processes.

As is usual with an ongoing process, the team chose to run a multi-vari study to investigate patterns of variation in the covers. The multi-vari study looked at within-piece variation, cavity-to-cavity variation, cycle-to-cycle variation, short-term time-to-time variation, longer-term time-to-time variation, and machine-to-machine variation.

The results of the multi-vari study on the visual defects showed mostly time-to-time variation, while the important dimensional characteristics indicated mostly cavity-to-cavity variation. These results clearly separated the corrective action needed into two categories: corrective action for visual defects and corrective action for excessive dimensional variation. The visual defects variation (time-to-time) related to process variables such as temperature, time, and pressure. The dimensional variation primarily involved the construction of the individual cavity. The size of each cavity determined what dimensions would be made in that cavity. Differences in dimensional characteristics were built into the cavities. Therefore, adjusting process variables such as mold temperature or injection pressure did not significantly affect the dimension.

Reducing Dimensional Variation

If a cavity was damaged and then replaced, there was a new "machine" (actually, a new process) producing parts with different dimensions. The cavities could not all be made exactly the same but the team found that the cavity-to-cavity dimensional variation was more than expected and more than should be allowed. The corrective action for the excessive dimensional variation focused on reworking or replacing problem cavities.

Correcting Visual Defects

To determine the proper process variable settings for eliminating visual defects, the team designed and ran an experiment called a *process latitude* or *tolerance analysis study.* The purpose of the latitude study was to determine if the process specifications were correct. The process variables in the experiment were forming pressure, holding pressure, temperature profile, pin cooling temperature, and cavity cooling temperature. All five process variables were run at two levels, low and high. The team set the low and high test levels at the limits of the currently accepted process variables (e.g., lowest permitted cavity temperature and highest permitted cavity temperature) to determine what effect the full range of these variables had on the various visual characteristics. The specification limits of the variables were used because these were the process variation ranges that normally occurred.

In a designed experiment with five variables each at two levels, there are 32 (i.e., 2^5) test conditions. Sixteen of the 32 conditions were run and from this study the team was able to determine what the specifications should be. This is a fractional factorial designed experiment—½ of 2^5. A classic fractional factorial experiment was appropriate to use because the team was interested in these five variables only and was certain the key variables were included in them.

Of the five variables, one was found to have a moderate effect and one had a drastic effect on the visual defects. The variable that produced a drastic effect had specification limits that were too wide, so the team narrowed the specification and retested to determine more realistic limits. In contrast, the team found that the remaining three variables had little or no effect on the visual defects even though the process limits were tested. The team was able to substantially widen the specification limits for the three variables after retesting. These new, wider specification limits simplified processing, thereby saving time and money without having a negative effect on the visual characteristics.

The key variables in this case history are intentionally not identified to the reader. In other situations the effects or interactions of other process variables such as make or type of molding machine, amount and type of additives or fillers in the raw plastic (e.g., stearates, glass fiber, etc.), percentage of reground plastic, mold design, and so forth will be different from those in this case study. What is important is that two process variables caused the overwhelming majority of the visual defects in this case study and those two variables were identified by the problem-solving team so that appropriate corrective action could be taken.

Conclusion

In this case, the manufacturer's problem involved complaints of excessive dimensional variation and visual defects in the product. To resolve the problem, the team:

- Determined that the sampling procedure previously used did not fit the actual process conditions.
- Developed a system so that visual defects could be rated numerically. The new sampling procedure considered which cavities produced the parts being measured. The samples were selected so that, over a period of time, products would be selected from all cavities on a scheduled basis.
- Ran a multi-vari study to determine the patterns of both dimensional and visual defects variation.
- Ran a fractional designed experiment to pinpoint the causes of the visual defects.

The results of the multi-vari and designed experiment studies showed that:

- Attempts to force corrections in dimensions by changing process variables such as temperature or pressure were not successful and might only make the problem of visual defects worse.
- Certain cavities had to be reworked or replaced to reduce the amount of overall dimensional variation to acceptable limits.
- One process variable had to be respecified to narrower limits to eliminate the problem of visual defects, but

three variables were set to wider limits to make processing easier.

The Case of Rejects on a Multicavity Compression Molder

Step 1—Provide focus. Some customers were complaining about visual and/or dimensional defects.

Step 2—Get close to the problem. A problem-solving team took a close look at the multicavity-forming machine.

Step 3—Quantify the output. The dimensional characteristics were already properly measured. The team created a numerical scale for rating each visual defect.

Step 4—Run multi-vari study(ies). The team investigated the process with a multi-vari study considering variation within piece, cavity-to-cavity, cycle-to-cycle, short-term time-to-time, longer-term time-to-time, and machine-to-machine.

Step 5—Design experiment(s). A designed experiment was not required for the dimensional characteristics because the multi-vari study solved the problem. For the visual defects, a five-factor experiment was designed considering forming pressure, holding pressure, temperature profile, pin cooling temperature, and cavity cooling temperature.

Step 6—Turn the problem on and off. Regarding dimensional defects, correcting the cavities corrected the problems. Regarding the visual defects, changing specification on four of the five factors allowed the problem to be turned on and off. One specification was tightened and three were opened up.

Step 7—Optimize. The results from the designed experiments allowed specifications to be set. Tests at specific levels permitted the team to optimize the process.

Step 8—Install process controls on key variable(s). The process controls were to rewrite the specification on four of the five variables tested and to create specifications for cavities.

Step 9—Measure before and after results. The incidence of dimensional and visual defects was drastically reduced.

Chapter 12

The Case of Varying Seat Measurements

The following case involved excessive variation in an important characteristic called a seat dimension of a forged part. The seat dimension is formed in a forging press and is crucial for further processing. In this case, inconsistent seat dimensions had led to processing problems, and an in-house cross-functional team comprised of the engineer, quality controller, and production foreman had been assigned the job of solving the problem. The problem was not affecting the ultimate customer, but was creating considerable problems a few operations later. It was negatively impacting internal customers.

The manufacturing operation started with the operator placing 30 parts in a tray and then setting the tray on a rotating table in an oven. The heated parts were extremely hot and sat near the opening of the oven. The operator used tongs to pick them up, one at a time, and place them into the forging press. The operator then forged each one, dropped it into a container, and returned for another. By the time the operator picked up the last parts, they had cooled quite a bit with the air drawn past them into the oven accelerating the cooling process.

The engineer maintained that the seat dimension variation was caused by excessive cooling. He felt that it was necessary to devise a method to keep the parts at a constant hot temperature to avoid the problem. He had begun work on a constant temperature device that would involve design, procurement, and installation time as well as incur expenses. However, the engineer believed that this device would solve only part of the problem.

The engineer felt that the operator caused much of the problem by placing the parts in the forging press inconsistently. Because the operator worked piecework, he or she ran them in and out of the forging press quickly and did not take the time to position each one carefully. Therefore, the engineer had also begun designing a device that would hold the part in the forging press at the "correct" distance. The estimated cost of this device was $30,000 and it would have taken about six months to build. The engineer felt this second device would solve the rest of the problem. His strategy was a typical example of blaming the operator and then designing out operator influence.

In order to expedite problem-solving efforts, an outside investigator was called in to assist the in-house team. The investigator began by asking the engineer how the seat dimension of each part was measured and learning that a vernier caliper was used to measure across the middle of the seat. The investigator explained that when a vernier caliper is used a burr or flash from the forging operation can result in an inaccurate measurement. He suggested that a pointed micrometer would be more accurate because a burr or flash would not be measured. The engineer agreed, so the measurement system was changed.

The Multi-Vari Study

Once the more accurate measurement system was in place, the investigator suggested running a multi-vari study. The engineer and investigator agreed to measure each seat in three places—the top, the middle, and the bottom of the forged area—to study within-piece (within-part) variation. To study part-to-part variation, the investigator chose to measure five parts in a row. It was also decided that the first and the last five parts would be taken out of a tray in order to study any effect of temperature. The study was scheduled to be run during the first and second shifts to determine time-to-time and shift-to-shift variation. Before the study began, the engineer stated, "I really don't like to run tests when I already know the answer." The investigator assured him that if the data proved consistent with the engineer's own hypothesis, he could use these results to convince others of his case.

The operator and quality controller started the multi-vari study by measuring the first five parts in a row in the tray and the last five in a row in the tray. The results from 10:30 A.M. are shown in Figure 12-1. By the time the first five readings were plotted, the investigator asked the engineer if he realized that the die was faulty. The investigator stated, "You're supposed to be making a parallel unit. The top and middle dimensions are very close to being the same, but the bottom dimension is much larger due to the shape of the die." The engineer replied, "Yes, the way they hand grind the dies that could easily happen." After the last five readings from the first tray were plotted, the investigator noted that, "The first five and the last five have very little difference between them. It doesn't seem

Figure 12-1. Seat Dimension Multi-Vari Study— Comparison of First Five Parts to Last Five Parts.

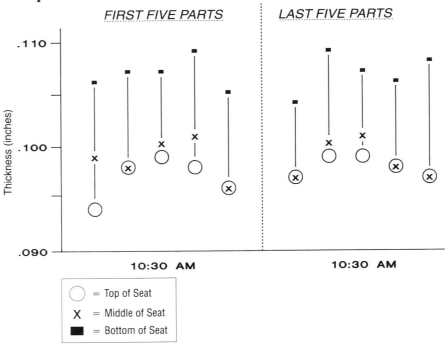

that sitting and cooling in the tray makes much, if any, difference."

Figure 12-2 shows the time-to-time variation. The dimensions of the five piece samples were averaged so the time-to-time variation throughout the day could be more easily detected. Measurements are also made during the second shift, which started at 3:30 P.M., so shift-to-shift variation could be seen as well. When the measurements of the first five parts are compared to the last five from a given tray, it is quite clear that temperature, within the range that was being tested, made no significant difference. The main difference lay in the thickness of the bottom versus the top and middle of the seat. Some

Figure 12-2. Seat Dimension Multi-Vari Study—Time-to-Time Variation.

time-to-time variation occurred, but it was small in comparison to the within-piece variation. The engineer was reluctant to accept the fact that the temperature did not make any difference and noted that the effect of placement in the forging press had not been tested. "Possibly the operator, who had the quality controller watching him, placed all the parts in the forging press about the right distance. We are obtaining this $30,000 device to ensure that the operator will always put them in properly," the engineer commented.

The Designed Experiment

The investigator and engineer then decided to design an experiment to test the effect of the varying distances of the parts within the forging press because the multi-vari study had ruled out temperature as a key variable and demonstrated that the greatest variation was within piece. A designed experiment was used because the investigator and engineer had to intentionally change the distances the operator placed the units in the forging press. Each tray contained 30 parts so it was agreed that 10 would be placed in the forging press at the right distance, 10 "in too far," and 10 "not in far enough." The order of running the designed experiment was selected by using a random number table.

The results of the designed experiment are shown in Figure 12-3. The top and middle of all seat dimensions averaged 0.098 inch. Whether the parts were in too far, at the correct distance, or out too far, essentially location made no difference in the results of the designed experiment. It is rare for industrial data to be so consistent. The major variation was within the part, the same result as had been obtained earlier. The engineer asked the quality controller if he had made sure the operator put the parts both in too far and not in far enough. The quality controller answered that he had decided to run the experiment himself and knew it had been done correctly. The engineer finally agreed that location in the press made no difference. By examination, the investigator found that those pushed in too far had flash on the back, while those not

Figure 12-3. Results of the Designed Experiment.

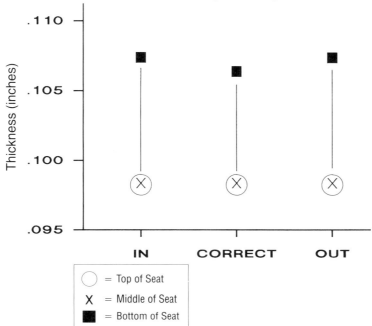

pushed in far enough had flash on the front. The only difference caused by distance into the forge was the location of the excess flash, which would be trimmed anyway. The cavity in the die determined the dimensions and the operator did not influence the results in any significant way.

However, the engineer was still reluctant to accept the idea that temperature made no difference. Since the quality controller admitted that it had taken him much longer to run the tray of work than it would have taken an operator, the effect of temperature on the results was again examined. The data were replotted, comparing the first 10 parts forged (the hottest ones) with the "middle" 10 and with the last 10 (the least hot ones). Figure 12-4 shows the results with the top, middle, and bottom readings averaged together. The figure clearly indicates that the temperature had no significant effect on the size of the seat even when the amount of cooling was greater than the parts would have experienced when a skilled operator performed the job.

Figure 12-4. Average Seat Dimensions Show Little
Variation Even After Substantial Cooling.

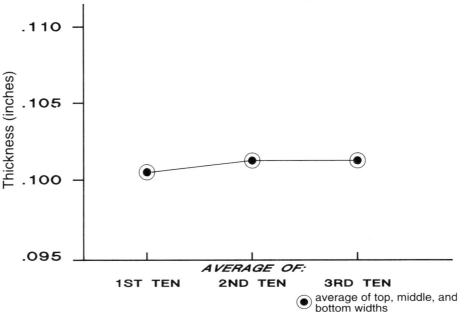

Conclusion

This case illustrates that "an ounce of data is worth a ton of opinions." The traditional Observe, Think, Try, Explain method did not work. To find the cause of the problem, the investigator needed valid data from a properly designed, carefully run, accurately plotted, and correctly analyzed key variable isolation study. However, even though the combination of a multi-vari study and a designed experiment eliminated the first two guesses—temperature and placement in the die—and zeroed in on the key variable—the size of the die—the implications were greater than that. In this typical factory situation, for example, if the engineer had been pressed for results, he would have responded that a few months and $30,000 later a new design would be in place and the problem would disappear. Unfortunately, time and money would not have resolved the situation. The procurement and installation of the two devices that the engineer wanted would not have corrected the problem, would have cost thousands of dollars, and would have further delayed identifying the true source of the excessive variation.

The Case of Varying Seat Measurements

Step 1 — Provide focus. Inconsistent seat dimensions were creating considerable processing problems a few operations later.

Step 2 — Get close to the problem. The team showed the investigator the two major steps in the process, heating the parts in an oven and forging to size in a forging press.

Step 3 — Quantify the output. The vernier caliper that was in use could distort reading if a burr from a previous operation or flash from the forging operation got in the way. A pointed micrometer replaced the vernier caliper. The team decided to take measurements at the top, middle, and bottom of each seat.

Step 4 — Run multi-vari study(ies). The team ran a multi-vari study considering within-piece variation (three locations on the seat), piece-to-piece, beginning to end of tray of heated parts, time-to-time within shift, and shift-to-shift. The multi-vari study eliminated temperature as a cause and highlighted an unsuspected cause, a miscut die.

Step 5 — Design experiment(s). The team designed, ran, and evaluated an experiment that clearly confirmed the suspected cause and eliminated operator placement as a possible cause.

Step 6 — Turn the problem on and off. The problem was completely eliminated when the die was repaired.

Step 7 — Optimize. Once the problem was eliminated, optimization was not required.

Step 8 — Install process controls on key variable(s). By eliminating the problem, process controls were not necessary.

Step 9 — Measure before and after results. The high incidence of processing problems dropped to zero.

Chapter 13

The Case of Bore Defects on Centrifugal Castings

While a problem-solving team was working with a foundry that centrifugally cast cylinder liners, the company's management asked the team to investigate a bore defect problem. The team first met with all key personnel and gave them the opportunity to suggest the causes of the problem. A meeting of this type is important because it assures everyone that management considers the solution to a problem to be a high priority.

The problem involved a visual defect that had not been previously quantified. Thus, the problem-solving team's next step was to devise a system for quantifying the defect. The team developed the following numerical rating scale:

> 0 — No Defect
> 1 — Minor Defect, Not Rejectable
> 2 — Major Defect, Barely Rejectable
> 3 — Rejected for Large Defect
> 4 — Rejected for Huge Defect

The Multi-Vari Study

Using this scale, the team then ran a multi-vari study. The company had six centrifugal casting machines. Three operators were employed to run these machines—each operator running two machines. The team inspected three consecutive castings from each of the six machines (i.e., 18 castings were inspected) at each of six different times during the day as shown in Figure 13-1.

Figure 13-1. Tabular Results of the Multi-Vari Study.

OPERATOR		A		B		C		AVERAGE DEFECT SCORE	CARBON CONTENT
MACH. #		5	10	9	8	7	6		
1	9:15	0 0 0	0 0 0	0 0 0	0 0 0	0 0 0	0 0 0	0.00	3.06
	9:30	0 0 0	0 0 0	2 2 0	0 0 0	2 0 2	1 2 1	0.67	3.19
2	11:25	3 2 1	1 2 2	2 2 2	2 2 2	3 3 4	1 1 4	2.17	3.43
	11:45	1 1 2	3 1 2	2 1 2	2 1 1	1 2 1	1 1 3	1.56	3.43
3	2:55	0 0 0	0 0 1	0 0 0	0 0 1	0 0 0	0 0 1	0.17	3.12
	3:10	0 1 0	0 0 1	1 1 4	3 3 1	1 2 1	1 1 3	1.33	3.34
AVERAGE DEFECT SCORE		0.61	0.72	1.11	1.00	1.22	1.17		

While carbon content was one suspected cause of the problem, to intentionally change the carbon levels would have been a difficult task. Therefore, the team initially chose to simply record the carbon content during the multi-vari study. The intention of the study was to look for excessive within-casting variation, casting-to-casting variation, operator-to-operator variation, casting machine-to-casting machine variation, short-term time-to-time (20 minutes) variation, and longer-term time-to-time variation within the day.

Figure 13-1 shows the results of the multi-vari study. The three numbers in each block are the defect scores for each of the three consecutive castings. The column averages indicate that for all three operators the variation between their two centrifugal casting machines was very small, 0.61 versus 0.72, 1.11 versus 1.00, and 1.22 versus 1.17. The largest variation between operators was less than two to one, 1.22 + 1.17 (total, 2.39) versus 0.61 + 0.72 (total, 1.33). However, the average defect scores by time show great variation between the first two times (0.00 at 9:15 A.M. and 0.67 at 9:30 A.M.) and the next two times (2.17 at 11:25 A.M. and 1.56 at 11:45 A.M.). From these results the team determined that looking for excessive within-casting variation would not be useful.

The multi-vari study indicated: (1) insignificant casting machine-to-casting machine variation; (2) operator-to-operator variation of less than two to one; (3) large time-to-time variation; and (4) defect scores correlating somewhat with carbon content—the higher the carbon content, the higher the defect score. However, these conclusions did not explain the variation between the 11:25 A.M. (avg. 2.17) and 11:45 A.M. (avg. 1.56) results when the carbon level remained the same at 3.43%.

Next, the problem-solving team focused on the significant time-to-time variation. The team asked what could vary within 20 minutes to cause such an abrupt change in the level of bore defects. At 11:25 A.M. there were two 4's and none at 11:45 A.M.; at 11:25 A.M. there were only four 1's while at 11:45 A.M. there were ten 1's out of the 18 castings. The team felt that temperature was a prime candidate for the cause of the rapid changes.

The Designed Experiment

For the multi-vari study the problem-solving team had selected stratified samples and then had "let the process do the talking." The process provided two strong clues—that carbon content and another variable, possibly temperature, were causing the defects. The next step was to design an experiment in which the team could intentionally vary factors to test its theory. The team chose to run three temperatures—"hot," "medium," and "cold," which represented the center and extremes of the normal operating temperature range. The team selected five levels of carbon content, recognizing that it would be difficult to control the carbon content exactly. Concerned about other variables that possibly could change with time, the team randomized the order of running the 15 combinations of temperature and carbon content.

The importance of randomizing cannot be overemphasized. If the team had not randomized but instead had run all the "cold" metal first, then the "medium" metal, and finally the "hot" metal, any differences in results would have been attributed to differences in metal temperatures when it could have been some unknown factor varying with time. Some engineers resist the need for randomizing. For instance, when running tests with varying temperatures there is a great temptation not to randomize because of the extra time it takes to change to the new temperature, particularly to a lower temperature.

The team chose to run three consecutive castings in each block or set of conditions to look at casting-to-casting variation. It made sense to take more than one casting at each level because it took so long to stabilize each condition. (Statistically speaking, these three castings were repeats, not true replications, because they were selected consecutively and were not produced by returning to the same set of conditions three times.)

Figure 13-2 shows the data from the designed experiment.

Figure 13-2. Results of the Designed Experiment.

CARBON CONTENT	METAL TEMPERATURE			AVERAGE DEFECT SCORE
	HOT	MEDIUM	COLD	
3.06	1 1 1	0 0 0	0 0 0	0.33
3.08	1 0 2	0 0 0	0 0 0	0.33
3.12	0 1 1	0 2 2	0 0 0	0.67
3.17	2 2 1	1 2 0	0 0 0	0.89
3.19	1 3 3	1 2 1	0 0 0	1.22
AVERAGE DEFECT SCORE	1.33	0.73	0	

As the carbon content increased from 3.06% to 3.19%, the average defect score increased from 0.33 to 1.22, a fourfold increase. However, as the temperature increased from "cold" to "hot," the average defect score increased from 0.00 to 1.33. These data indicated that going from "cold" to "hot" (within the range of testing) had a much greater effect on defect score than going from a low percentage of carbon to a high percentage of carbon (within the range of testing). From these two conclusions, an investigator might assume that high temperature/high carbon was the worst condition, and, indeed, the lower left corner of Figure 13-2 is the worst block. Also, it might be assumed that the best block would be the low temperature/low carbon block, and, in fact, the upper right corner of Figure 13-2 is all 0's. However, all 0's appear not only in the upper right corner but also in the entire right column where the temperature was "cold." In addition to depicting the effects of carbon level and temperature, this visual analysis provided a third conclusion. If the metal was poured "cold" enough, carbon (within the range of testing) did not have an effect on the defect score. To describe the effect of carbon content on the defect score the team had to say, "It depends on the temperature," which means that an interaction was involved.

There were a number of practical implications to understanding the two key variables, carbon content and temperature, and also the interaction between them. The team concluded that the problem could be solved by keeping both temperature and carbon content low. On the other hand, the process could be made less sensitive to variation in carbon content with better temperature control—and temperature was easier to control than carbon content.

For further clarification, Figures 13-3 and 13-4 show the main effects of the key variables, carbon content and temperature, each plotted on the same average defect score scale. Note that the plots of both of the graphs increase from lower left to upper right, further indicating that defect scores increase as temperature and carbon content increase.

The effect of the interaction between carbon content and temperature on the defect level is shown in Figure 13-5. This

Figure 13-3. Average Defect Scores vs. Carbon Level.

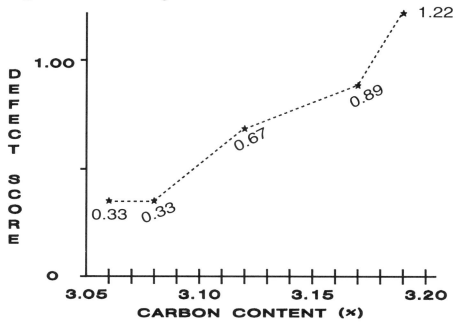

Figure 13-4. Average Defect Scores vs. Metal Temperature.

Figure 13-5. Interaction Effects.

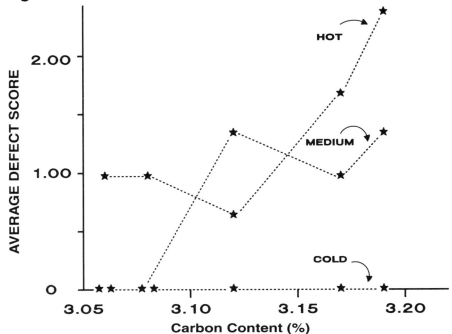

figure uses the data derived from the averages of the three-piece individual-defect scores shown in Figure 13-2. Note that the plots of the defect levels for the medium and hot temperatures are erratic and tend to slope upward while the plot of the defect levels at the low temperature is a horizontal line at zero defects. Figure 13-5 reflects a nonparallel response. A nonparallel response indicates the presence of an interaction. The effect of the carbon content on the results depends on what the temperature is.

The Case of Bore Defects on Centrifugal Castings

Step 1—Provide focus. Management knew that bore defects was one of their top customer problems.

Step 2—Get close to the problem. The problem-solving team visited the area where the centrifugal castings are produced.

Step 3—Quantify the output. This visual defect had not been previously quantified. The team devised a 0 to 4 numerical rating scale—an important step.

Step 4—Run multi-vari study(ies). The multi-vari study considered within-casting, casting-to-casting, operator-to-operator, machine-to-machine, short-term time-to-time, and longer-term time-to-time within the day. The multi-vari ruled out a number of the potential types of variables and highlighted suspected variables, temperature and carbon content.

Step 5—Design experiment(s). The team used the knowledge from the multi-vari to design an experiment with the two apparently most important variables.

Step 6—Turn the problem on and off. The team could turn the problem on and off by adjusting the two key variables.

Step 7—Optimize. The designed experiment included areas where there were zero defects and where the temperature of the process was not sensitive to carbon levels. Therefore, further optimization was not necessary.

Step 8—Install process controls on key variable(s). New temperature limits were established and monitored and carbon content was continually measured.

Step 9—Measure before and after results. The incidence of this visual defect went from one of the top customer problems to zero.

Chapter 14

The Case of Weeping Stoppers

By Thomas S. Woods

A Pareto analysis had shown that leaks were the most serious defects in the molded stoppers that a company manufactured. These stoppers were made of a new type of material, and, if the incidence of leaks could be reduced substantially, the company had high hopes for the success of the product. A management task force assigned to solve the leak problem decided to use the key variable isolation strategy and named a three-person team to undertake the job. The team included the design engineer for the project, the production supervisor, and a process engineer.

Stoppers were first tested under field conditions. During this testing, the stoppers were inserted into a circular glass opening of a special container, simulating the neck of a bottle. Pressure then was applied to a liquid inside the container, and the team observed the neck and stopper to see if any drops of liquid escaped. Stoppers that showed drops, or "tears," were referred to as "weepers." Although this method was adequate for determining whether a given stopper leaked, it did not provide sufficient information about the severity of an individual leak so that the team could discriminate between various levels of leakers.

To obtain more information about the stoppers, the team tried several methods of improving quantification. Quantification is crucial to solving problems of this nature—it is extremely difficult to analyze data when most of the scores are zero. Eventually, the team settled on a multi-vari study involving overstress testing, which used a level of liquid pressure higher than that used in the first test. When defect rates are low, overstress testing can be useful. For the overstress testing, the liquid inside the container was colored red so that the team could measure the area of the red stain that appeared on a piece of white blotting paper applied to the outside of the stopper. The overstress test provided a distribution of scores, and patterns of variation soon became apparent.

The Multi-Vari Study

The multi-vari study showed that the variation in the amount of leakage past the stopper was greatest between stoppers molded in successive cycles of the same mold. The team agreed with the design engineer that the variables that fit the "cycle-to-cycle" category were material plasticity, mold temperature, and the amount of stearate lubricant used. Each of these variables had been investigated individually in a number of previous experiments but the results generally had been inconclusive. Moreover, when these experiments were repeated, the results often turned out to be entirely different from the results achieved the first time. However, the engineer hoped that the current testing might reveal some new information.

At first, the location of the leaks appeared to be random with respect to the orientation of the stopper. However, when the location of every leak was plotted on a measles chart of the mold, it appeared that nearly two-thirds of the leaks occurred in the portion of each stopper that was made opposite the inlet where the molten plastic was injected into each cavity. Closer examination of the worst leakers then showed that the location of the leak was sometimes associated with the location of a nearly invisible "knit line" or seam in the stopper where the melted plastic flowed together in the cavity. When this knit line ran vertically along the sealing surface of the stopper from bottom (inside the bottle) to top (outside the bottle), it could provide a passageway for liquid to escape.

The Designed Experiment

Based on the analysis of the multi-vari study the team designed a three-variable, two-level experiment to determine the relative importance of each of the three variables—plasticity, mold temperature, and lubricant level—on leakage. The first step of this experiment was to lay out the experimental design as shown in Figure 14-1 and to determine the two levels of operation for each variable. These levels were set to represent conditions near the extreme high and low levels of typical operation for each variable. Variable A, plasticity, was given a value of 7 for "low" and 12 for "high." Variable B, mold temperature, was set at 300°F for "low" and 340°F for "high." Variable C, lubricant level, was set at "normal" or "high" levels of stearate lubricant based on the spray time.

The second step of the experiment was to determine the

Figure 14-1. Designed Experiment Layout Grid.

		PLASTICITY A			
		"7" −		"12" +	
		LUBRICANT LEVEL C		LUBRICANT LEVEL C	
		NORMAL −	HIGH +	NORMAL −	HIGH +
MOLD TEMPERATURE B	300°F −	CELL 1	CELL 2	CELL 3	CELL 4
	340°F +	CELL 5	CELL 6	CELL 7	CELL 8

number of replicate runs to be made under each set of conditions. Because of production schedules and the time and cost of running the experiment, a decision was made to use the minimum number of trials needed to get a measure of interaction—two mold cycles for each of the eight cells, or sets of conditions, for a total of 16 cycles. (If the results of this "minimum" run turned out to be inconclusive, then a third and even fourth replicate could have been run at a later date.)

The third step involved determining the sequence in which the trials were to be run. Because there were eight cells (as shown in Figure 14-1), eight playing cards (ace through eight) were placed in a box and randomly drawn out one at a time to determine the sequence of the first run of eight mold cycles. The first card drawn was the deuce, so that the first cycle would be run under the conditions shown in cell 2. Cell 2 shows Variable A as $(-)$, or 7; Variable B as $(-)$, or 300°F; Variable C as $(+)$, or high. When all the cards had been drawn, they were again shuffled, placed in the box, and drawn to determine the sequence of the next run. The results of this "randomization" drawing are shown in column two of Figure 14-2. Columns three, four, and five list the conditions for the three variables for each of the tests.

The fourth step was to make the stoppers in the random sequence shown in Figure 14-2. The fifth step was to test the stoppers. All the stoppers were marked and then randomized before testing, to avoid any systematic bias in the test procedure.

Test Results

Results of the tests are shown in the right-hand column of Figure 14-2 and in the designed experiment grid shown in Figure 14-3. For example, stoppers made in the first trial run under the conditions described in cell 2 produced leakage with a total area of 17—shown circled in Figure 14-3. The remainder of the right-hand column of Figure 14-2 indicates the results for the other 15 cycles.

The designed experiment was analyzed using an analysis

Figure 14-2. Test Schedule and Results of the Designed Experiment.

CYCLE	CELL NUMBER	CONDITIONS			STAINED AREA
		A	B	C	
1	2	−	−	+	17
2	5	−	+	−	15
3	8	+	+	+	17
4	6	−	+	+	25
5	7	+	+	−	13
6	3	+	−	−	16
7	4	+	−	+	06
8	1	−	−	−	24
9	6	−	+	+	12
10	1	−	−	−	21
11	4	+	−	+	17
12	7	+	+	−	06
13	5	−	+	−	23
14	8	+	+	+	26
15	3	+	−	−	20
16	2	−	−	+	09

of variance (ANOVA) program, which measures the effect of all variables and their interactions in relation to the residual error. The results shown in Figure 14-4 indicate that plasticity was not a significant variable and that although mold temperature and lubricant level on the average did not affect the amount of weeping, there was a strong interaction between those two variables (B and C). Whether or not a variable or interaction is significant is determined by comparing the confidence level to a predetermined limit. In this example it was decided before the data were analyzed that if any effect (variable or interaction) exceeded the 90% confidence level it would be considered significant. Only the BC interaction exceeded

Figure 14-3. Designed Experiment Results Grid.

			PLASTICITY A			
			"7" −		"12" +	
			LUBRICANT LEVEL C		LUBRICANT LEVEL C	
			NORMAL −	HIGH +	NORMAL −	HIGH +
M O L D — T E M P E R A T U R E	B	300°F −	24 21	(17) 9	16 20	6 17
		340°F +	15 23	25 12	13 6	17 26

Figure 14-4. Results of the ANOVA (Analysis of Variance).

FACTOR	SUMS OF SQUARES (SS)	DEGREES OF FREEDOM (DF)	MEAN SQUARE (MS)	F RATIOS	CONFIDENCE LEVEL
A	39.06	1	39.06	1.091	67.2%
B	3.06	1	3.06	0.086	22.7%
C	5.06	1	5.06	0.141	28.4%
AB	0.06	1	0.06	0.002	3.3%
AC	60.06	1	60.06	1.677	77.0%
BC	189.06	1	189.06	5.279	95.1%
ABC	22.56	1	22.56	0.630	45.5%
Residual	286.50	8	35.81		
TOTAL	605.42	15			

A = PLASTICITY   B = MOLD TEMPERATURE   C = LUBRICANT

this decision limit, with a confidence level of 95.1%. This interaction is plotted in Figure 14-5, first with mold temperature (Variable B) plotted at both lubricant levels and then with lubricant level (Variable C) plotted at both mold temperature levels. An interaction plots as a nonparallel response. In Figure 14-5, the plots intersect—an indication of a strong interaction.

Figure 14-5. Interaction Plots—Leakage Scores vs. Test Conditions.

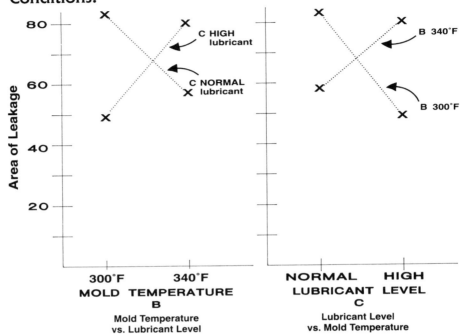

(While in this case the two graphs actually provide the same information, in many studies, cross-plotting data can reveal important clues.)

To describe whether the mold temperature had an effect on weepers, the team had to say that it depended on the lubricant level. When the mold temperature increased from low to high the weeping score went down, if the lubricant level was normal. But the weeping score went up as mold temperature increased if the lubricant level was high (see the left-hand graph in Figure 14-5). This interaction was the reason the design engineer had obtained inconclusive and even contradictory results during earlier testing.

As Figure 14-6 indicates, the worst combinations occurred when the mold temperature was low and the lubricant level was normal (a score of 81), and also when the mold temperature was high and the lubricant level was high (a score of 80). The scores in Figure 14-6 are derived from the data in Figure

Figure 14-6. Summary of Leakage Scores for B and C
Conditions.

		MOLD TEMPERATURE B	
		300°F −	340°F +
L U B R I C A N T — L E V E L — C	NORMAL −	81	57
	HIGH +	49	80

14-2. For example, the score of 81 in Figure 14-6 comprises the scores where condition B is (−) and C is (−) without regard for condition A. These numbers—16, 24, 21, and 20—total 81.

The team's conclusion was that running the operation at the low mold temperature (300°F) and at the high level of stearate lubricant would provide the widest safety margin against weepers. The second best combination, mold temperature at 340°F and stearate lubricant at normal level, would also provide an adequate safety margin against weepers. Either combination could be chosen depending on ease of operation and economic factors.

The Case of Weeping Stoppers

Step 1—Provide focus. A Pareto analysis showed that "weepers" were the most serious defect.

Step 2—Get close to the problem. A three-person team showed the investigator the process of making the stoppers.

Step 3 — Quantify the output. This step was a crucial one because the previous testing indicated only good stoppers and the occasional weeper. The team developed an overstress test and an ingenious way of measuring the amount of weeping.

Step 4 — Run multi-vari study(ies). The multi-vari study considered within-piece variation due to mold cavity-to-cavity, cycle-to-cycle or shot-to-shot, mold-to-mold, machine-to-machine, batch-to-batch, shift-to-shift, and day-to-day.

Step 5 — Design experiment(s). The team agreed that the pattern of variation identified on the multi-vari study agreed with three potential variables. The team designed an experiment to test these three variables, each at two levels. The designed experiment clearly identified an unsuspected two-factor interaction.

Step 6 — Turn the problem on and off. The team adjusted the levels of these two interacting variables, and the level of weepers varied both in numbers and degree of weeping.

Step 7 — Optimize. This case history is a classic example of where optimization is important. By using three levels of the two variables that are interacting, optimum conditions can be determined.

Step 8 — Install process controls on key variable(s). Once the optimum conditions are determined, normal process controls can be applied to ensure that the two key variables are controlled as well as practical.

Step 9 — Measure before and after results. This problem that had been at the top of the Pareto chart was now eliminated.

Chapter 15

Introduction to Isoplots

An isoplot is a graph that can be used to compare two sets of results, numbers and measurements. The comparison of the two sets of data can be used to monitor quality trends, to audit the output of a process, to quantitatively describe the relationship between one variable and another, to evaluate problem-solving techniques, and so on.

Creating an isoplot starts with gathering the two sets of data and arranging them in a tabular form. Figure 15-1 shows two hypothetical sets of data, called A and B, arranged side by side. The data in the left-hand column—set A in Figure 15-1— are considered the standard or reference data and the data in the right-hand column—set B—are considered the observed or measured data and are the data that will be compared to the standard data.

To compare the data on the isoplot, the two sets of data are plotted as coordinate points on a graph. For example, in Figure 15-1 the first pair of numbers is 1 and 2. To plot the corresponding point for these two numbers, one would move

Figure 15-1. Data Table.

A	B
1	2
2	3
3	4
4	5
5	6
6	7
7	8

one unit to the right along the X-axis (the horizontal axis) and two units up the Y-axis (the vertical axis) as shown in Figure 15-2. To place the second point (2, 3) on the graph, one would move two units along the X-axis and then three units up the Y-axis, as shown in Figure 15-3. The complete graph of the data in Figure 15-1 is shown in Figure 15-4.

A 45-degree line of perfect agreement (perfect correlation) is usually shown on isoplots. If the observed data were exactly the same as the standard data, the plotted points would fall on the 45-degree line; actual data, however, are virtually never perfect and virtually never plot this way. In actual use several types of graphs may occur:

• The plotted points may fall on a (more or less) straight line but not the 45-degree line, as is the case in Figure 15-5. In this case the observed data are referred to as *biased* or *inaccu-*

Figure 15-2. **Plotting the First Point.**

Figure 15-3. Plotting the Second Point.

*rate.** This type of plot often occurs when an uncalibrated measuring instrument, such as an uncalibrated micrometer, is used to obtain measurements.

  • The plotted points may cluster around and on both sides of the 45-degree line as shown in Figure 15-6. In this case the observed data are often referred to as *imprecise.*

  • The plotted points may "cloud" as shown in Figure 15-7. This type of plot results when there is no relationship between the standard and observed data or when the measuring equipment or technique is hopelessly unsuited to the task.

*In this chapter, the terms *bias* (or *biased*), *inaccurate,* or *imprecise* are used only to mean that the observed data do not agree perfectly with the standard, or expert, data. Because all "real-life" observed data are to some degree biased or imprecise, no attempt is made to define when data are *too* biased or *too* imprecise. That decision in actual practice must be made under the constraints of the use to which the data and evaluation will be put.

Figure 15-4. Complete Graph.

Using the Isoplot

Suppose that in an actual factory setting a scale of 1 to 8 is set up to evaluate visual defects on a product. Suppose also that a team of experts has evaluated 40 samples of the product and has agreed on a numerical rating to be assigned to each product item as shown in Figure 15-8. The company now wants to determine how closely the quality control inspector's numerical rating of these same 40 items will agree with the experts' rating. The inspector's evaluation of the items is shown in Figure 15-9. (Note that the item numbers shown in the left-hand column bear no relationship to the numerical rating assigned to the item either by the experts or by the inspector.)

The first step in creating the isoplot that will be used to compare the two sets of data is to arrange them in tabular form as shown in Figure 15-10. The coordinate points are shown in ascending numerical order. After the data have been com-

Figure 15-5. Biased Data Isoplot.

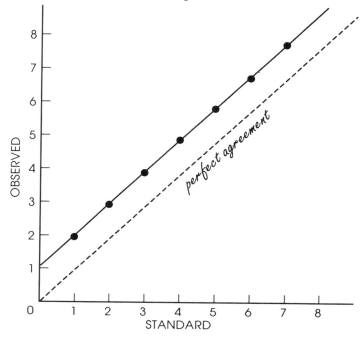

piled, the coordinate points are plotted as shown in Figure 15-11. A typical point plotted is that of the experts' rating (2) and the inspector's rating (3); this point is circled.

Now that the isoplot is complete, a measure of the inspector's level of accuracy can be established by defining *accuracy* as the percentage of points on or within one division (as measured along the X- or Y-axis) of being on the 45-degree line. Of the 40 coordinate points, all but 5 are on or within one division of being on the line. Therefore, 35 out of 40 points are *accurate* and the accuracy rating is 87.5%. A more stringent method would be to count only those points that are on the 45-degree line. In Figure 15-11, 20 points would be on the line of perfect agreement and 20 would be off the line, a 50% accuracy.

A measure of *bias* can be determined by counting the direction and amount the inspector's readings are away from the 45-degree line and by summing the above-line (plus) scores, summing the below-line (minus) scores, and obtaining the algebraic total. In Figure 15-11 this calculation is $(13 - 12) =$

Figure 15-6. Imprecise Data Isoplot.

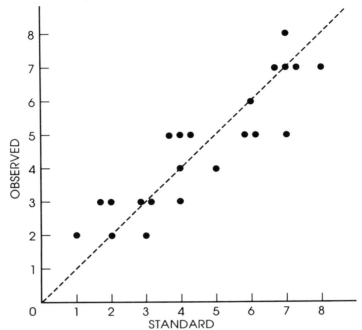

+1. Dividing +1 by 40 results in a bias rating of +2.5%. If the algebraic total were a negative figure, there would then be a negative bias.

If a company wanted to determine how well a group of observers agreed with the standard/experts, isoplots could be made for each individual and the agreement then determined on a consensus basis. Accuracy and bias could also be collectively calculated.

Figure 15-7. Clouded Data Isoplot.

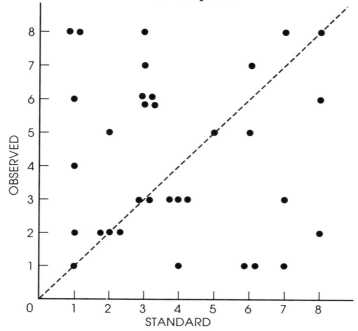

Figure 15-8. Experts' Rating Table.

Item Number	Experts' Rating	Item Number	Experts' Rating
1	②	21	2
2	1	22	6
3	1	23	4
4	3	24	3
5	5	25	5
6	1	26	4
7	3	27	7
8	2	28	2
9	4	29	6
10	1	30	5
11	4	31	7
12	4	32	4
13	6	33	3
14	3	34	8
15	8	35	6
16	3	36	4
17	5	37	5
18	7	38	3
19	4	39	8
20	5	40	5

Figure 15-9. Inspector's Rating Table.

Item Number	Inspector's Rating	Item Number	Inspector's Rating
1	③	21	2
2	1	22	8
3	2	23	4
4	3	24	4
5	4	25	5
6	1	26	4
7	1	27	7
8	2	28	4
9	4	29	7
10	1	30	4
11	3	31	7
12	5	32	3
13	7	33	2
14	3	34	8
15	6	35	6
16	1	36	5
17	5	37	4
18	8	38	3
19	4	39	8
20	6	40	5

Figure 15-10. Coordinate Point Table.

Item Number	Experts' Rating	Inspector's Rating	Item Number	Experts' Rating	Inspector's Rating
2	1	1	26	4	4
6	1	1	12	4	5
10	1	1	36	4	5
3	1	2	5	5	4
8	2	2	30	5	4
21	2	2	37	5	4
1	2	3	17	5	5
28	2	4	25	5	5
7	3	1	40	5	5
16	3	1	20	5	6
33	3	2	35	6	6
4	3	3	13	6	7
38	3	3	29	6	7
14	3	3	22	6	8
24	3	4	27	7	7
11	4	3	31	7	7
32	4	3	18	7	8
9	4	4	15	8	6
19	4	4	34	8	8
23	4	4	39	8	8

Figure 15-11. Isoplot of Product Ratings.

Isoplot of Product Ratings

Note: In some cases coordinate points may not be placed exactly upon the values shown in Figure 15-10. The dotted lines parallel to the 45-degree line are one division from the line.

Chapter 16

The Case of
the Noisy Motor

By Art Leason

A top-of-the-line manufacturer had enjoyed high consumer regard for its product for several decades. With time, the product had undergone minor alterations as new materials became available and as the company's manufacturing concept changed and developed. The energy crisis and high consumer acceptance led to the use of the product in more critical situations than the designers originally had planned for. Eventually, complaints began to surface concerning a noisy component of the product: an electric motor. The complaints were followed by a slow but steady increase in warranty costs. New competition began to enter the field. After some months the negative effects of warranty costs and leveling sales were reflected in the company's profit margin.

The search for solutions began in the traditional manner. Company management questioned manufacturing and motor design about what had changed and what might be going wrong. Manufacturing responded by showing that minor changes, each one by itself seemingly insignificant, had over a period of time developed an almost totally different electric motor. Motor design insisted that if manufacturing followed the specification limits the motor would work properly. These specification limits, however, had not been followed to the letter for years. Thus, the stage was set for a war of words and much finger pointing. At this point the problem-solving team was contacted and began working on an approach that would resolve the situation.

The Multi-Vari Study

After looking at the manufacturing operation, the problem-solving team began with a multi-vari analysis of the motor. As a part of the multi-vari analysis, the following numerical rating scale for the noise was created:

    0   No Detectable Noise
    1   Barely Detectable Noise
    2   Noise Clearly Present but Acceptable
    3   Noise Too Loud to Accept
    4   Gross Noise

The investigation proceeded with noise tests being performed on eight motors in a row in the morning, again at midday, and toward the end of the shift. Noise tests at those three periods were repeated the following day. The results are shown in Figure 16-1. The inspector who performed the tests said there

Figure 16-1. Results of the Multi-Vari Study.

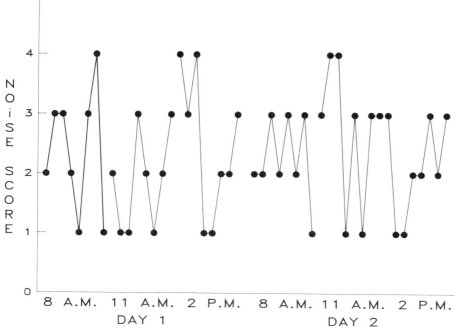

seemed to be a difference as he moved around the motor and thus the noise appeared to move. However, the best that could be done at that time was to score the total motor.

Figure 16-1 shows a large unit-to-unit (i.e., motor-to-motor) variation, but little time-to-time or day-to-day variation. Unit-to-unit refers to motors made consecutively. It was believed that a within-unit (within-motor) score could not be obtained. This belief was a crucial flaw. If it is not possible to measure one of the main categories of variation, that category may identify the key variable.

The investigators agreed with the inspector that the amount of noise and its location within the motor seemed to change relative to the listener's position. The investigators then wondered whether, if the noise "moved" within the motor, could the noise "move" between motors. To answer this question, four motors at each noise level (1, 2, 3, and 4) were randomly presented to the inspector and were measured a second time. The results are graphed in Figure 16-2a. All the plot-

Figure 16-2. Isoplots of Noise Measurements.
PERFECT CORRELATION PLOTS ON THE 45° LINE

First Score
vs. Second Score

First Inspector
vs. Second Inspector

ted points would have been on the 45-degree line if there had been an exact agreement between the measurement of each motor the first and second time. (This 45-degree plot is called an isoplot.) Instead, Figure 16-2a demonstrates little agreement between measurements. The same 16 motors were then given to a second inspector. In Figure 16-2b, the plot compares the first reading of the first inspector against the first reading of the second inspector. This plot does not show good agreement either. Figures 16-2a and 16-2b indicate that the same inspector did not obtain a similar result on retesting the motor nor did two inspectors agree on what the reading should be. The analysis is difficult because there is confounding among:

- Motor behavior (Is the motor changing?)
- Measuring (listening) ability (frequency and amplitude variations)
- Other (interaction with other components such as motor mounting)

An attempt was made to train the listener/inspector. Repeatable and reproducible measurements still could not be obtained. Components such as bearings, armatures, and brushes were switched but repeatability and reproducibility continued to elude the investigators.

Management agreed that the multi-vari analysis and isoplots clearly demonstrated the need for an improved measuring method. In addition, considering the amount of money being lost in warranty costs, management believed that it would make sense to invest in an objective measuring system if one could be found or invented. The project paused while a sound-level measuring device was located and purchased and the investigators learned to use it. In addition, an anechoic room (an acoustically insulated room with low reverberations) was constructed to house the motor being measured. The measuring system consisted of the anechoic room where a motor being analyzed was hung from a TV antenna rotor in front of a sound spectrum analyzer microphone. The antenna rotor was used to physically change the position of a motor relative to the microphone. The motor could be turned through 360 degrees and an integrated sound measurement taken over 32 segments. The within-unit measurement then consisted of 32 readings that were 11.25 degrees apart.

When the noise measurement, anechoic room system was in place, a multi-vari test of the within-unit noise levels was performed on a typical motor. Figure 16-3 shows a plot of the noise level for all 32 segments along with a sketch of the motor testing layout. From the study, a clear pattern of within-unit variation emerged. What had looked like motor-to-motor variation was nothing more than the results of the random position of the motor in relation to the listener. After concluding that there was only slight motor-to-motor variation, the investigators concentrated on within-unit (within-motor) variation. The next step was to determine why there was within-unit noise variation. Then the problem could be corrected.

Figure 16-3. **Within-Motor Noise Levels of "Typical" Motor.**

The potential list of a very large number of process variables had been cut by two-thirds through recognition that the primary type of variation was within-unit—not unit-to-unit or time-to-time. The type of variation—within unit—that was not captured in the first multi-vari study proved to be the one that involved the key variable.

Evaluating the Clues

The sound spectrum analyzer used in the test allowed the investigators to measure a motor and mark a quiet location and a noisy location within it. After a motor was marked, it was disassembled and measured to find the correlation of noise and dimension. Much to everyone's surprise, this dimensional analysis did not lead to an elegant and simple explanation of the cause of the noise. Although within-unit clues found by the sound spectrum analyzer were confusing, they pointed to concentricity and the relationship between the stator and rotor as contributing to the noise problem. Therefore, an "old model" motor was constructed using old components still in customer service inventory and assembled using the old procedure as best as it could be reconstructed. The results were spectacular. The "old model" was quiet and had almost no within-unit variation, as shown in Figure 16-4.

Dimensional analysis showed that the stator and rotor were smoother and more concentric than current model motors, information that the company already knew. The company had previously made a decision to allow "rough" laminated stacks to be used in the stator and rotor in order to save money. This change had been checked and was found to be acceptable. However, the method used to check the change could not be confirmed, as formal test reports had not been made.

Nevertheless, the clue that the old model motor was smoother and more concentric was pursued by building a very special new motor and rotor with adjustable concentricity. This was accomplished by making small changes in concentricity in the metrology laboratory. The concentricity of the sta-

Figure 16-4. Within-Motor Noise Levels of "Old Model" Motor.

tor to the rotor is measured in total indicator reading (TIR). Figure 16-5 shows the within-unit variation with a stator where the TIR of the concentricity was adjusted to 0.0060 inch. The average sound level of 50.0 decibels (db) was too high to be acceptable and the within-unit variation was significant. By using an improved stator alignment with a TIR of 0.0050 inch, an improved sound pattern had an average noise level of 48.2 db. The press for improvement continued. A further reduction of TIR to 0.0022 inch reduced the average noise level to 44.5 db.

Figure 16-6 shows the results when TIR had been held to 0.0015 inch—the average noise level was 42.8 db and there is little within-unit variation.

Figure 16-7 shows an excellent relationship of db (noise level) to TIR: as TIR was reduced, the noise level went down. Not only had the key variable—excessive nonconcentricity of the stator and rotor—been isolated but also a relationship, as shown in Figure 16-7, had been established, indicating that the

Figure 16-5. Within-Motor Noise Levels—0.006-Inch TIR.

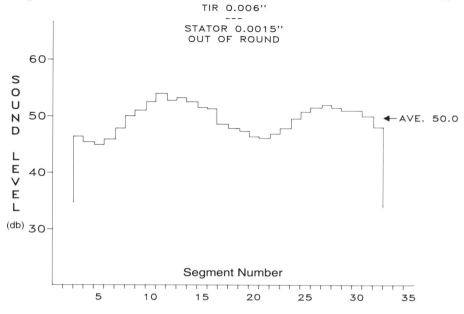

Figure 16-6. Within-Motor Noise Levels—0.0015-Inch TIR.

Figure 16-7. Relationship of Noise Level to TIR.

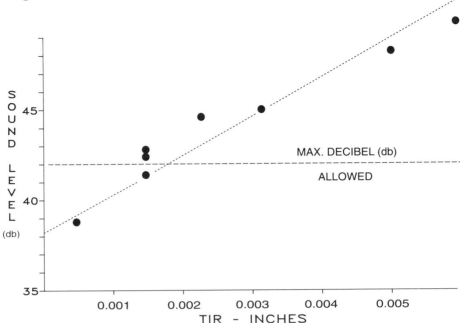

motor noise was a function of the amount of nonconcentricity, as measured in TIR. The mystery of the noise had been solved. The results showed that when the existing specifications were followed, the motor was too noisy. This was a clear case of allowing specifications to grow more lenient until they no longer reflected the levels needed for customer satisfaction.

This case demonstrates the power of multi-vari analysis in problem solving and the necessity of having an adequate measuring method. Multi-vari analysis provided a way to partition the problem, reject whole groups of process variables that had nothing to do with the problem, and focus on clues that led to a solution.

The Case of the Noisy Motor

Step 1—Provide focus. Customer complaints about noise and warranty costs were increasing and profit margins were reflecting these adverse trends.

Step 2—Get close to the problem. A problem-solving team looked at the operation and also the specifications.

Step 3—Quantify the output. The team created a numerical rating scale for noise from 0, no detectable noise, to 4, gross noise.

Step 4—Run multi-vari study(ies). The team ran a multi-vari study considering motor-to-motor, time-to-time within day, and day-to-day. Little benefit was obtained, so a new listening device was developed to study within-piece (motor) variation.

Step 3—Quantify the output. Because the multi-vari study clearly indicated a need for a better measuring system, a new measuring system was developed.

Step 4—Run multi-vari study(ies). With the new measuring system the multi-vari study clearly showed that within-unit variation was the major pattern of variation.

Step 5—Design experiment(s). A designed experiment was not required; the combination of multi-vari and a good quantification system solved the problem.

Step 6—Turn the problem on and off. The team turned the problem on and off conveniently.

Step 7—Optimize. Plotting the correlation between noise level and the nonconcentricity was the optimizing step.

Step 8—Install process controls on key variable(s). The specifications were changed to keep the decibel level of the motor below a maximum allowed level.

Step 9—Measure before and after results. Before the study, customer complaints and warranty costs for motor noise were increasing. After the study, customer complaints and warranty costs for motor noise disappeared.

Chapter 17

The Case of Low Yield on Solid-State Devices

By John Pollard and John M. Reddy

A high-tech Silicon Valley company making solid-state devices was considering reducing operations at one of its satellite plants. The company had ample justification for this decision: Profits had waned, competition had stiffened, and management felt the need to back the winning operations and abandon the losers. In addition, the plant, while in relatively good order, did not meet the standards of the company's most critical customers. A prevailing belief was that at the very least a portion of the plant would have to be rebuilt.

Before the company made a final decision on the future of this plant, however, management asked a problem-solving team to review the operation. Following the strategy of first seeking out strengths upon which to build improvements, the team identified several pluses in the operation. The team found that the plant management and staff knew the technology of the process and the product. An eager workforce operated the modern equipment efficiently and testified to their willingness to seek improvements. In addition, the company had a strong customer list. Many companies would find these enviable assets. However, the company's process yield typically ran only about 35%—that is, for every unit shipped, almost two units did not meet specifications. Most of the losses were for low electrical strength. Even with a highly favorable environment—no union, low labor cost, nominal overhead—this plant could not return a profit.

At the time the problem-solving team performed its review, plant operations were based on the following policies and beliefs that made it difficult to improve yields:

1. The root of problems lay in the operators not following instructions. Therefore, only more training and discipline could improve yields.
2. Each day the company was required to review every operation for conformance. Any departure would automatically call for immediate corrective action.
3. It was required that proposed improvements be checked out one at a time.

These policies and beliefs might be useful if applied to some basic manufacturing operations, but this company's solid-state processing involved 42 steps and hundreds of process variables. Normal processing time was about eight weeks. The idea of individually exploring the effects of improvements one at a time could not be used effectively in this complex process.

To approach these problems the team used a technique called **random balance,** developed during the 1950s by Dr. Frank Satterthwaite, a mathematician. Random balance is a type of stratified sampling that selects specific random paths through the process to examine the contribution of each variable. While this method can be complex in detail, following the random balance line of reasoning as it applied to this solid-state manufacturing company's processes was a fascinating exercise in cryptography—much like the deciphering of a secret code. Dr. Satterthwaite based his reasoning on two basic ideas: sampling theory and the maldistribution theory (Pareto concept).

Sampling Theory

According to sampling theory, if there are major differences between items in a large lot, a relatively small random sample can determine the presence of these differences. The sample size is only slightly influenced by the lot size. Maximum efficiency is reached for a sample size of 30 to 50. A great deal of information is gained for each unit increase in sample size up to about 30, while increases beyond 50 yield a decreasing improvement in knowledge about the lot.

The purpose of a screening test such as random balance is to find the presence of any key variables, the effects of which, based on the Pareto concept, should stand out clearly. In the same way, if a random sample of combinations of process variables is tested, the key variable(s) should stand out.

Pareto Concept

The Pareto concept suggests that whenever differences exist there are one or more forces in action creating these differences. Even the slightest action, such as the arrival of the operator at his or her machine, has an effect—perhaps too small to measure, but still a contribution. The total number of variables contributing even the smallest amount to the total variation in a product can be very large.

Obviously, all elements do not make an equal contribution to the total effect. Experience supports this statement, and when the list of possible contributing variables is large enough, the effect of each contribution ranges from quite small to significantly large. Of the contributors only a few are generally responsible for a half or more of the total effect. Thus, the Pareto concept involves the maldistribution (unevenly distributed) principle.

If all contributions could be ranked according to their effect, a Pareto chart, such as in Figure 17-1, would result. In this figure, which represents an earlier and perhaps more traditional method of Pareto charting, each column represents the "remaining percentage" of the causes of excessive variation or other process problems. For example, the far left-hand column indicates that of the total variation 23% is attributable to cause B (shown shaded) and 77% to all other causes. The second column indicates that of that remaining 77%, 22% (shown shaded) is attributable to cause C. In turn, of the remaining 55%, 16% (shown shaded in the third column) is at-

Figure 17-1. Traditional Pareto Chart.

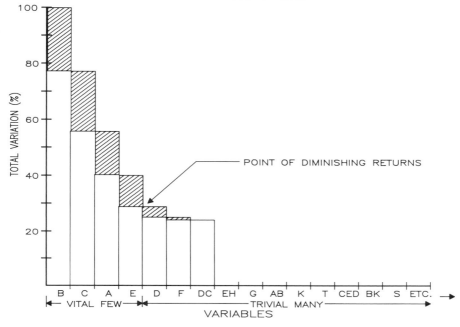

tributable to cause A. Causes B, C, A, and E, then, account for about 71% of the total variation or causes of the problem.

When the effect is variation, the Pareto concept becomes even more important. Well-known statistical relationships prove that random variation adds by the sum of the squares rather than by straight addition because it is highly unlikely that all variables will be at the level contributing the most (or least) variation at any given time. For example, using only two variables to describe the principle, if one variable contributes six units of variation and the second only one unit, the total process variation V is:

$$V = \sqrt{6^2 + 1^2} = \sqrt{37} = 6.1$$

The major contributor has such a large, overriding influence that totally eliminating the small variable has an insignificant effect on the results. For example, if the variable contributing one unit of variation in the above example were removed, the new total variation would be as follows:

$$V = \sqrt{6^2 + 0^2} = \sqrt{36} = 6.0$$

which is only slightly different from when the one unit of variation was also affecting the result.

A useful way to combine these two concepts—sampling theory and the Pareto concept—is to consider the magnitude of an individual effect, that is, variation, contributed by each variable, as the elevation of mountain peaks, hills, and bumps. In a region of few peaks and many small hills and bumps, if the highest peaks—"the vital few"—are removed, what is left appears relatively level and the removal of one more hill or a few bumps—"the trivial many"—changes the topography an insignificant amount. In real-life situations, this is the point at which the removal of the largest remaining contributor to the problem brings little practical benefit. It is often referred to as the point of diminishing returns. At this point, the removal of small effects does little to reduce the total variation. It does little good to locate and remove large numbers of small hills and bumps, if even one large peak remains.

By combining sampling and maldistribution theories, Dr. Satterthwaite developed the random balance design for experimentation. His resulting strategy is a method for screening all possible significant contributing variables in a limited number of test runs. The strategy's primary objective is to locate the peaks—that is, the key variables—through a rough screening system. If 20 possible contributing variables were put into a random balance designed experiment, almost certainly the important peaks among the 20 would be located. It can be assumed that the maldistribution of causes of a given effect exists and that only a very few of the contributing causes have major effects while the large majority have minor and relatively insignificant effects. This assumption is borne out by considerable practical experience.

Random balance was developed from an earlier type of screening test, the fractional factorial designed experiment. However, to obtain the benefits of fractional factorials, the testing requires rigidity in its planning and execution. Also, it becomes difficult to keep the number of test runs low as variables are added and still keep balance, particularly when more than two levels of variables are needed. The fractional factorial design is most efficient as long as it requires 30 or fewer test sequences. Random balance does not have this limitation and therefore is more efficient when the number of variables to be studied requires more than 30 test sequences.

The random balance design does not limit the number of variables that may be programmed into an experiment. If 20 variables include all the "vital few" peaks, then it does little harm to add another 10 or so variables to the experiment since they must be in the category of the "trivial many." The real peaks will continue to protrude.

All significant variables should be included in the experiment to achieve the screening objective. Other unprogrammed variables will be reflected in the residual variation that the analysis examines. If the analysis is done sequentially, as the experiment is performed, test results will indicate the likelihood that any significant variables have been overlooked and permit the addition of newly suspected variables in the design after the experiment has started. Therefore, the random balance experiment—especially with its ability to add variables during the experiment—presents far greater flexibility than the more rigidly planned fractional factorial experiments.

Example of Random Balance

An example of a random balance experiment follows. The example involves a simplified situation in which the engineers believe that there are only six variables that are affecting process yield. Four of these variables, A through D, are to be tested at three different process settings (levels). The symbol "+" represents the process setting at the highest practical level that in the judgment of the engineers is acceptable in making a good product. The symbol "o" is used for the average level and the symbol "−" is used for the lowest practical level. For the remaining two variables, E and F, the engineers agree that testing only at the highest and lowest levels is appropriate. They decided on 30 tests, the minimum number of data points for variables analysis.

The layout of the experiment and the results are shown in Figure 17-2. Note that test R1 is a replicate of test 6 and R2 is a replicate of test 19 in order to confirm repeatability. The total of test runs in the example, therefore, is 32.

In this example variables A through D have three levels, so to maintain balance there are 10 tests at each of the three levels. For variables E and F there are 15 tests at each of the two levels. A random number table is used to determine the order of running these tests. Replicate tests are not included in the definition of balance. While the test layout is truly random, it is also balanced by maintaining the same number of tests at each of the levels. This is a form of stratified sampling, which helps in simplifying the analysis.

Analysis of Example Test Data

After completing the 32 test runs a plot of yield was made in the order of testing to check whether any unusual pattern of results existed that might suggest some unknown, time-dependent influence on the test results. The test results were sufficiently random to ensure that no major unknown time-associated factors were influencing the results in any systematic fashion. It should be noted that the replication runs (6 and R1, 19 and R2) showed very good agreement when compared to the overall variation of yield figures.

A random balance experiment is analyzed by making scatter plots of the results. The scatter plots of the six variables are shown in Figure 17-3. Note that there are 10 points (plus the results of any replicate tests) shown in each plot for each test condition. The data for each of these points come from the test results of each test condition shown in Figure 17-2. For example, each of the points shown for A− in the upper left-hand plot of Figure 17-3 corresponds to a result for which variable A had a low (or " − ") value in Figure 17-2. To highlight the effect of each variable, the difference between the median readings for the two levels that produced the highest and lowest yields is marked on the scatter plots (see Figure 17-3). The four key variables in descending order of importance based on the numerical difference between the high and low median values

Figure 17-2. Random Balance Test Layout and Results.

TEST LAYOUT AND RESULTS (YIELD)

TEST RUN #	A	B	C	D	E	F	RESULTS
1	o	−	o	+	−	−	58
2	o	o	−	o	−	+	38
3	−	+	−	+	−	−	04
4	−	−	+	−	+	+	92
5	o	+	+	−	−	+	.73
6	+	−	−	o	+	−	76
7	+	o	o	+	+	−	66
8	−	o	−	−	+	−	28
9	o	−	o	−	+	+	56
10	o	+	−	o	−	+	08
11	+	+	o	−	+	−	69
12	+	o	+	−	+	+	82
13	+	−	+	+	−	−	78
14	o	−	+	o	−	+	71
15	−	o	o	−	+	−	46
16	−	o	o	o	−	−	44
17	−	+	−	o	−	−	02
18	o	o	o	+	+	−	55
19	+	+	−	+	−	+	24
20	−	o	+	+	+	+	61
21	o	+	−	−	+	+	44
22	−	−	+	+	+	−	92
23	+	−	o	o	+	+	94
24	+	+	+	o	+	+	83
25	o	o	+	+	−	−	66
26	+	+	−	−	+	+	54
27	−	+	o	o	−	−	16
28	−	−	−	+	−	+	30
29	+	−	o	o	−	−	64
30	o	o	+	−	−	+	71
R1(See #6)	+	−	−	o	+	−	75
R2(See #19)	+	+	−	+	−	+	26

Figure 17-3. Scatter Charts of Test Results.

and the best setting for each are: B−, C+, A+, and E+. From the data alone, the highest yields could be predicted, with reasonable confidence, by combining these four variables at the level that gives the highest results even though this combination was not tested.

Analysis of Solid-State Process Data

Applying this random balance technique to the solid-state process mentioned earlier in the chapter is somewhat complicated by the many process steps and length of time it takes to process one silicon wafer. The justification for all the extra work is that when 50 wafers are processed using a random balance design, it is then possible to decode the entire process and identify the critical areas for further exploration.

The initial test run in the plant in question included not six variables as outlined in the example but 15 variables. The orientation and location of each silicon wafer in each process step was also recorded by the technicians. In addition, the electrical strength of each of the 200 or so devices on each of the 50 wafers was recorded. With 50 wafers there were 50 tests run instead of 30 as in the generic example explained earlier in the chapter.

The engineers could then observe the actual pattern of results within each wafer as well as the overall yield. The details of any random balance test run may appear complicated, but the process engineers within their own process are easily able to keep track of what happens. The engineers, after all, have lived with the many steps in even the most complicated processes.

Three trials over a six-month period showed exactly what had to be done to make consistent product. The answers did not relate to the workforce, plant cleanliness, or process upsets—the issues addressed by plant management. The solutions provided by the process itself revealed vast differences in the quality of incoming material. In addition, certain process equipment inherently could not make a consistent product, all of which was compounded by incorrect and incomplete specifications for several process steps.

The proof, of course, lay in the results of this process analysis. By implementing the findings from the studies, yields of 85%, rather than 35%, were realized. Senior management reversed itself on the future of the plant and considered the plant one of its most significant assets. Plant management began to manage the process by consulting the process itself.

Multiple Balance

An upgrade of the random balance test design is a multiple balance test design in which groups of two, three, or four variables are laid out in a full factorial test design while the remaining variables are randomly assigned. The way the variables are grouped is based on engineering judgment and past experience as to which variables are most likely to interact with each other. As with any screening test, using knowledge and experience is a great aid. With this strategy, the groups of two, three, or four variables can be analyzed as full factorial test designs while all the other variables are treated as "noise" or residual error. As in the random balance designs, scatter plots are used to analyze all variables.

The Case of Low Yield on Solid-State Devices

Step 1—Provide focus. The yield for the plant was only about 35%, competition had stiffened, and profits had waned. The plant did not meet the standards of the company's most critical customers. Management considered closing the plant.

Step 2—Get close to the problem. A problem-solving team reviewed the operation and looked at the 42 steps in the process.

Step 3—Quantify the output. There already existed a good output measurement, electrical strength.

Step 4—Run multi-vari study(ies). The random balance test design was used without running a multi-vari study.

Step 5—Design experiment(s). The team used a random balance designed experiment format with 15 variables and ran 50 tests to decide the real contributors to variation.

Step 6—Turn the problem on and off. When the corrections suggested by the random balance experiment were implemented, the yield improved dramatically.

Step 7—Optimize. Optimization was obtained by setting all 15 variables at the preferred level.

Step 8—Install process controls on key variable(s). The process was controlled by changing the process specifications to the levels indicated by the test results.

Step 9—Measure before and after results. Before the study the plant yield was 35% and management considered closing the plant. After the results of the study were implemented, yields of 85% were realized. Management considered the plant one of its most significant assets.

Chapter 18

The Case of Improving Aluminum Die-Casting Quality

By Robert W. Traver With Gregory Brown

A company wanted to improve the quality of one of its key products, an aluminum die-cast part used by the automotive industry. To achieve this improvement, the company decided to hire industrial investigators who were recommended by a major customer. The company was a preferred supplier, but the customer had become increasingly concerned about the quality level of the aluminum part.

The Quality Improvement Program

The investigators began their program for quality improvement with a one-day training session in the strategies and techniques of statistical process control (SPC) and key variable isolation. SPC training presented ways of using fundamental statistical concepts to measure and control excessive variation in a manufacturing process. Key variable isolation training helped the company's engineers to identify sources of variation that were missed by or unavailable to traditional problem-solving methods.

The program was structured around four longstanding problems that arose in the manufacture of die-cast aluminum products. These problems involved: (1) casting, (2) cleaning, (3) machining, and (4) maintaining the plane of a faced surface. Teams of three persons from different company functions were set up to deal with these problems. Though the problems differed in terms of specific details, each was successfully tackled using SPC and key variable isolation strategies and techniques. During the training, the team members received extensive coaching and practice. This training not only allowed them to participate in and contribute to the solution of the four problems, but also assured them the knowledge and experience necessary to solve, on their own, other product quality concerns.

Casting

The first quality improvement project dealt with the problem that had prompted the customer to recommend the investigators: too much porosity was present in one type of aluminum die casting when the castings were machined in the customer's plant. The improvement strategy called for creation of a numerical scale to rate the amount of porosity, a determination of the factors that caused excessive variation in porosity, and a plan to reduce or eliminate the factors causing this variation.

A scale of 0 to 5 was developed to quantify the degree of casting porosity. Porosity scores were determined by the size of a wire that could fit the pores. With these standards in place, all subsequent castings could be classified and compared. The score also supplied the numbers necessary for statistical and graphical analysis. An experiment was designed to determine the effects of two common variables that affect casting porosity: fast-shot length and fast-shot velocity. Two levels of fast-shot length—18 and 22 inches—and three levels of fast-shot velocity—40, 55, and 70 inches/second—were chosen to be tested during the experiment.

The designed experiment required the production of 12 separate castings, which were machined in-house in random order. After machining, the castings were carefully inspected and each of the six machined surfaces of each casting was rated according to the porosity scale. A measles chart of each casting was used to record the location and severity (0 to 5) of the porosity. Figure 18-1 is an example of one of these charts.

Figure 18-1. Measles Chart of Casting Defects.

To make the measles chart easier to read, the scores are shown on only two of the six surfaces (C and D) and only scores of 3, 4, and 5 are plotted. The circular casting was divided into eight sections to aid in the analysis of within-piece variation.

Results of the fast-shot velocity and fast-shot length experiment are shown in Figure 18-2. The main effects for the two variables are plotted using cumulative defect scores of porosity from the 0 to 5 scale. The plots clearly show that the lowest defect score occurred at the medium level of fast-shot velocity. Fast-shot length had very little effect on porosity within the range that was tested.

Following the fast-shot velocity and fast-shot length experiment, a second experiment was designed to test the effects

Figure 18-2. Results of the Designed Experiment.

of three different levels of fast-shot velocity on porosity. These levels were the medium velocity previously tested, a little higher, and a little lower. The objective of the test was to find the optimum level for the fast-shot velocity setting. The investigators looked for this level on both sides of the previously best level. To ensure that the experiment did not exclude any other important sources of variation, pressure was chosen as a second variable.

The results of the follow-up experiment showed that the optimum level for fast-shot velocity was a point a little lower than the original medium fast-shot velocity level. Pressure, within the range of testing, had a negligible effect. Before the testing, there was a concern that porosity was related to the distance from the gates. The measles chart clearly demonstrated that the porosity at the gates was essentially the same as between the gates (see Figure 18-1).

Where the optimum setting of fast-shot velocity was used, the defect level dropped drastically. It was now clear that while control of fast-shot velocity was crucial, controls over both fast-shot length and pressure did not need the attention they had been receiving. These last two specifications could be relaxed to save processing time and thereby increase productivity and save money.

Cleaning

The second project selected involved a tough cleaning problem. A large-size, large-volume aluminum die-cast part had strict cleanliness requirements for its interior surfaces, bored surfaces, and internal holes; the part wasn't clean enough. Before the project began, most educated guesses pointed toward the casting or machining steps of the manufacturing process as being responsible for "dirty" parts. Major contaminants—solder flakes, chips, dirt, and foreign material—originated during these steps. At the end of the manufacturing process, 25-unit lots of die-cast parts were examined by sampling and were either accepted for shipping or rejected and recleaned.

The cleaning project started with a review of the cleanliness specifications. These specifications limited the size of the individual particles, their total area, and their weight. The size was determined by removing the particles from the casting with a Freon flush, collecting the particles on a filter paper, and then, with a microscope, examining the particles on the filter paper using a reference grid. Weight was determined by a "before and after" weighing of the filter paper. Since the weight specification had never been exceeded, the primary concern was to reduce the quantity and size of the particles.

As in the casting project, the next step required the development of a numerical scale to rate particle area and size. A scale was created, based on the overall visual impression of the particles as they appeared on the filter paper. To develop the scale, five filters were chosen to represent different levels of casting contamination (see Figure 18-3). Each filter tested was then assigned a score ranging from 1 to 5 depending on which of the standards the filter most closely resembled. A perfectly clean filter, which never occurred, would have been rated a 0.

After the scale was developed, a multi-vari study was run. This study consisted of taking three consecutive castings following ultrasonic cleaning two or three times per shift, and the casting contamination level was rated. Important results appeared in just a few days. Figure 18-4 presents a plot of these results. The multi-vari study showed that casting-to-casting (piece-to-piece) variation and time-to-time, within-a-shift variation were negligible compared to the shift-to-shift variation that appeared. The piece-to-piece consistency and large variation in the cleaning process that appeared between shifts clearly pointed to the cleaning process as the key variable. This was an unexpected finding, but one clearly demonstrated by the multi-vari data. Further examination identified several

Figure 18-3. Numerical Rating of Casting Contamination.

Figure 18-4. Multi-Vari Study of Casting Contamination.

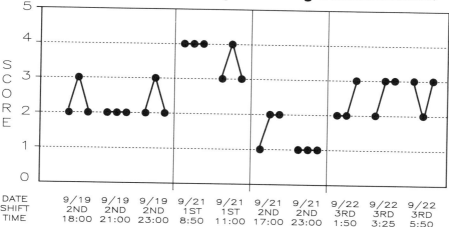

problem areas within the cleaning operation. Among these were that the washing water was not always kept sufficiently hot and sufficient wetting agent was not always used. The identification of these problem areas and the application of appropriate process controls to the cleaning operation brought casting cleanliness well within the required specifications.

Following the project, the simple filter inspection system to determine casting cleanliness and the numerical scale were maintained with a considerable saving in inspection time. Saving time was especially important because of growing production volume. Another result of the project was the removal of the lot-by-lot casting acceptance plan used prior to shipping and its replacement with a process control plan used at the end of the cleaning operation. This change virtually eliminated rejections and the saving in cleaning alone was substantial. Moreover, the customer received a cleaner, better product.

After a problem of this type is solved, it is often easy to say that better process control would have provided the answer. But this response fails to show how process control can determine which elements in the process are the most important and require the most attention. For example, before the study, process controls required frequent changes of rinse water in the ultrasonic cleaner. After the study it was found that rinse water changes were not important. Key variable isolation made it possible to identify the important and unimportant sources of variation in the process and thus determine where the greatest amount of control should be applied.

Machining

The third project dealt with a machining problem. One type of aluminum die casting had a very tight specification on the dimension from one hole location to the center line of a hole in another plane. The casting scrap rate for out of tolerance on this dimension on some runs had been 10% and even 20%. The problem-solving strategy called for the development of a procedure by which the hole-to-hole dimensional variation could be controlled.

Unlike the previous two projects, a usable, numerical scale in the form of a dial indicator reading was already available. Thus, step one was the running of a multi-vari study. To determine the major sources of variation, the multi-vari study examined the differences that appeared in the hole-to-hole dimension as a function of reading-to-reading (measurement repeatability), part-to-part, time-to-time within-a-shift, shift-to-shift, and day-to-day. When samples of five consecutive parts were graphed, it was clear that the most significant variation

Figure 18-5. Multi-Vari Study of Hole-to-Hole Dimension Variation.

was shift-to-shift (see Figure 18-5). This result meant that one operator had a better machining technique than the other. Excessive variation was eliminated when the preferred technique was taught to the second operator.

Another concern involved the larger-than-acceptable amount of variation that occurred with the use of the dial indicator gauge. This reading-to-reading variation indicated a lack of repeatability of the measurement. The problem was solved by purchasing a more precise (more repeatable) gauge. One of the suspected variables, temperature, contributed insignificantly to machining variation within the range that temperature varied in the factory.

Process Control

Following the identification of operator technique and gauge repeatability (precision) as the key variables in this machining problem, it was important to ensure that these variables be controlled. In this case, a *precontrol strategy** was introduced to guide the operator in making machine adjustments. Using precontrol resulted not only in better quality but also in fewer adjustments. The magnitude of the improvement was apparent when only two castings were scrapped in the next 1,600 produced. This level became the norm.

Precontrol is a sound, simplified method of establishing operator control of quality that:

- Indicates shifts in process centering.
- Indicates increases in process spread.
- Assures that the percent defective in the product will not exceed predetermined levels.
- Assures that inspection frequency can be adjusted to an economical level, making it ideal for long production runs.
- Assists with continuous improvement activities.

*For a thorough discussion of precontrol, see J. M. Juran and Frank M. Gryna, *Quality Control Handbook* (New York: McGraw-Hill Book Company, Inc., 1988).

In addition, precontrol:

- Requires no recording, calculating, or plotting of data. Plots can be made if desired. Thus, money is saved and it is more likely that the technique will be applied conscientiously.
- Can serve as a setup plan that starts with the first pieces produced. The technique is ideal for short production runs such as those often found in job shops.
- Works directly from the specification tolerances; data need not be accumulated to calculate control limits.
- Allows production to take advantage of the full specification tolerance. Precontrol does not try to control the production process more tightly than is necessary.
- Requires only simple instruction to use. Precontrol can be as basic as showing a "traffic light" comparison when the gauges have been colored.
- Can be used with attribute or even visual characteristics. Precontrol was originally developed as an attribute control plan. A separate set of gauges is used at the precontrol limits—the center half of the specification.
- Has as its target the center of the specification so that quality loss function is minimized.

Maintaining the Plane of a Faced Surface

The fourth quality improvement project focused on the evenness of the plane of the faced surface of an aluminum die-cast piston. Too many pistons were being scrapped because the faced surface was out of plane. An out-of-plane surface was determined by a two-step process. First, the castings were set on a three-point locator. Following basic rules of geometry, three points establish a reference plane. Then the contour of the surface around the circumference was measured in eight different places with a dial indicator capable of measuring to 0.0001 inch. This measurement provided a set of distances that indicated the degree to which various points on the piston plane circumferences varied from the reference plane.

The eight deviations could be plotted on a clock diagram,

which made it possible to compare the degree and location of out of plane from piston to piston. A clock diagram depicting a set of measurements is shown in Figure 18-6. (Note that had all eight points been in the same plane each point would have appeared on the zero axis—the dotted line—in the clock diagram.)

The next step was the multi-vari study. The study looked for the sources of the out-of-plane condition within piece by location, within piece before and after machining, piece to piece within a cast lot, and lot to lot. This information was obtained by comparing clock diagrams from the several pistons that were selected for measurement. The comparisons clearly demonstrated that the location of out of plane around

Figure 18-6. Clock Diagram of Piston Surface Variations.

the piston circumference was similar from piston to piston. This regularity strongly suggested that nonrandom sources of variation were at work in the machining step of the process. Supplied with this clue, the company's engineers scrutinized the machinery, in particular the chucking jaws.

What the engineers found supplied the solution to the out-of-plane problem. The chucking jaws did not apply an even pressure across the internal diameters of the casting and it was being "forced" out of plane. The engineers were able to document this deformation process by bluing the jaws, chucking a casting, and then looking for marks on the blued surface and changes in the clock diagram. To further demonstrate the mechanics involved, a paper model of the piston was developed and stressed in exactly the same manner as the aluminum part. Surface out-of-plane deformations that were identical to those on the part appeared on the model.

The problem was solved by modifying the chuck jaws and their positioning on the casting. The jaws were ground to make them concentric to the center of the chuck. In addition, the width of the jaws was decreased so that they contacted an internal diameter of the castings in line with the main casting structure, a position where the casting is strongest. This solution provided additional benefits when it was determined that it could be applied with little effort to a whole line of aluminum die-cast pistons.

Summary

Application of key variable isolation and statistical process control enabled the company to solve four of its longstanding quality problems. This resolution led to products manufactured with greater reliability and at a lower cost. For the company, the advantages of these problem-solving strategies were:

- In-house scrap and rework rates were lower.
- Scheduling was easier because of lower losses in a run.
- Production schedules could be met more quickly.

- Higher-quality, more consistent products were produced.
- Substantial savings in quality costs were obtained.
- Usable data were more easily obtained.
- Less frustration and better morale resulted.
- The company's technical expertise in die casting improved.

For the customer, the advantages were:

- Higher-quality, more consistent parts
- Better delivery schedules
- Lower scrap rates
- Dependable data when requested
- A better relationship with the supplier

The key variable isolation strategy as presented by the investigators proved to be a powerful problem-solving tool. However, the test of how well the strategy had been learned arose a few months after the completion of the formal consulting program. At that time, a major customer found that one of the company's products regularly failed an important quality test. The company's response was to apply the key variable isolation strategy it had recently learned. With this information, the problem was quickly diagnosed and corrected without outside help.

The Case of Improving Aluminum Die-Casting Quality

I. Casting

Step 1—Provide focus. This problem was the one that prompted the customer to recommend the investigators.

Step 2—Get close to the problem. The team observed the aluminum die-casting process.

Step 3—Quantify the output. The team developed a 0 to 5 numerical scale to quantify the amount of porosity.

Step 4—Run multi-vari study(ies). Essentially all castings had too much porosity. The two most likely variables were agreed on by the team so a multi-vari study was not done.

Step 5—Design experiment(s). The team designed an experiment with two variables, one at two levels and one at three levels. Results were plotted on measles charts, and then the totals were plotted on graphs.

Step 6—Turn the problem on and off. The degree of porosity could be altered by adjusting levels of the key variables, thereby turning the problem on and off.

Step 7—Optimize. After the designed experiment showed that the medium fast-shot velocity was the best of the three levels tested, optimizing tests were run just above and just below the previously best setting. The setting on the key variable was thereby optimized.

Step 8—Install process controls on key variable(s). The process was set to run at the optimum setting. Specifications on two of the previously suspected variables were relaxed, thereby saving processing time and increasing productivity and saving money.

Step 9—Measure before and after results. Before the study, the customer was quite concerned about the quality of this casting. After implementing the results of the study the defect level dropped drastically.

II. Cleaning

Step 1—Provide focus. Many lots needed recleaning, resulting in a high internal reject rate. A greater concern resulted from the customers' threat to stop buying unless the company could eliminate the "dirty" interior problem of this large-size and high-volume aluminum die-cast part.

Step 2—Get close to the problem. The cross-functional problem-solving team looked closely at the three major operations: casting, machining, and ultrasonic cleaning.

Step 3—Quantify the output. The lack of a consistent numerical reading for the amount of contaminates made this step crucial. The team developed a repeatable scale of 0 to 5.

Step 4—Run multi-vari study(ies). To detect patterns of variation, the team selected samples of three consecutive castings: casting-to-casting (piece-to-piece), two or three times per shift, shift-to-shift, and day-to-day. The pattern of data pointed to the cause of the problem.

Step 5—Design experiment(s). The multi-vari study discovered the problem and eliminated any need for designing experiments.

Step 6—Turn the problem on and off. Team members isolated the key variables and demonstrated their success by turning the problem on and off at will.

Step 7—Optimize. The team members skipped optimization since they had solved the problem.

Step 8—Install process controls on key variable(s). The team members established controls on the key variables. More specifically, they changed the control procedure from product lot acceptance to process control once they identified the key variables that needed control.

Step 9—Measure before and after results. Step 1 described the before results. Installation of the process control procedure that resulted from the study virtually eliminated rejects, saved considerable inspection time, and provided the customer with a cleaner, better product. This pleased the customer.

III. Machining

Step 1—Provide focus. There was usually a scrap rate of 10–20% on this casting after machining.

Step 2—Get close to the problem. The team observed the various machining operations involved in determining this dimension.

Step 3—Quantify the output. A dial indicator reading was already available.

Step 4—Run multi-vari study(ies). The multi-vari study considered differences due to reading-to-reading (measurement repeatability), piece-to-piece, time-to-time within a shift, shift-to-shift, and day-to-day.

Step 5—Design experiment(s). A designed experiment was not required because the multi-vari study pointed out the two key patterns of variation and pointed the direction for the corrective actions.

Step 6—Turn the problem on and off. When the two corrective actions were implemented the problem could be turned on and off.

Step 7 — Optimize. The multi-vari study pointed out the two things needed to correct the problem. Optimization studies were not necessary.

Step 8 — Install process controls on key variable(s). Precontrol was applied to this machining operation to center the process and keep results well within specification.

Step 9 — Measure before and after results. Before the team attacked this operation the scrap rate often was between 10% and 20%. After the two key variables were determined, corrective action was implemented, and precontrol was used, the typical scrap rate was 2 castings out of 1,600, or a scrap rate of approximately one-eighth of 1%. This is an 80- to 160-fold reduction.

IV. Maintaining the Plane of a Faced Surface

Step 1 — Provide focus. Too many pistons were being scrapped because the faced surface was out-of-plane.

Step 2 — Get close to the problem. The team looked at the operation and in particular the measurement technique.

Step 3 — Quantify the output. There was already a measuring system in place using a dial indicator that told the amount of out-of-plane to 0.0001 inch. However, the team members added a crucial refinement. They measured these out-of-plane readings in eight places around the piston and plotted the results on a clock diagram so the orientation of the out-of-plane could be related to the position in which the piston was being held in the facing operation.

Step 4 — Run multi-vari study(ies). A multi-vari study was run looking for patterns of variation within piece by location, within piece from before to after machining, piece-to-piece within a cast lot, and lot-to-lot.

Step 5 — Design experiment(s). The multi-vari study supplied the clues that were necessary for the engineers to solve the problem. A designed experiment was not needed.

Step 6 — Turn the problem on and off. The problem could be turned on and off by using the original chucking jaws on the machine and then the new chucking jaws.

Step 7 — Optimize. An optimization step was not needed.

Step 8—Install process controls on key variable(s). Modifying the chucking jaws eliminated the need for process controls.

Step 9—Measure before and after results. The corrective actions eliminated scrap for out-of-plane parts. The solution was then applied with little effort to a whole line of aluminum die-cast pistons.

The four examples in this chapter, along with the cases throughout the book, illustrate the application of the Traver Nine-Step Problem-Solving Process. These summaries clarify the following observations. Every case required the use of the following steps: Step 1—Provide Focus, Step 2—Get Close to the Problem, Step 3—Quantify the Output, Step 6—Turn the Problem On and Off, and Step 9—Measure Before and After Results. Step 4—Run Multi-Vari Study(ies) was used in almost all of the cases. The other steps only became necessary in some cases. Step 5—Design Experiment(s) sometimes served no purpose since the Multi-Vari Step had solved the problem. Step 7—Optimize was often not required because the variable or variables were eliminated. Optimization usually applies in process industries where there are processes with known variable(s) that have unknown optimal settings. Step 8—Install Process Controls on Key Variable(s) sometimes requires no more than elimination of the variable(s). Otherwise, a general control or a more formal statistical process control may prove necessary. These nine steps led investigators to solutions for all of the cases presented.

Chapter 19

The Case of Nondisintegrating Tablets

By Charles L. Rosen

A major pharmaceutical company had developed a new product. This tablet had been on the market less than a year when the production department began to experience difficulties in meeting outgoing quality specifications. The product could not pass the standard USP (United States Pharmacopoeia) disintegration test, which required that six tablets disintegrate within 30 minutes in 37°C water. If one or more tablets failed to disintegrate within that time, a second sample of 18 was tested, of which no more than one could take longer than 30 minutes to disintegrate. Failure of the product to pass this test and the resulting back-order situation were jeopardizing the company's new million-dollar product line.

Figure 19-1 outlines the manufacturing process steps for this product. First, raw material from an outside vendor was subjected to incoming quality control inspection. After inspection, the material was shipped to the formulation department where it was granulated, dried, and then batched with binders and other inert materials. The product moved on to the compression department where it was formed into tablets and coated. After coating, quality control performed final inspection.

Because the product moved through two organizational departments, quality control and manufacturing, and two functional departments within manufacturing, a problem

Figure 19-1. Tablet-Making Process Flow Chart.

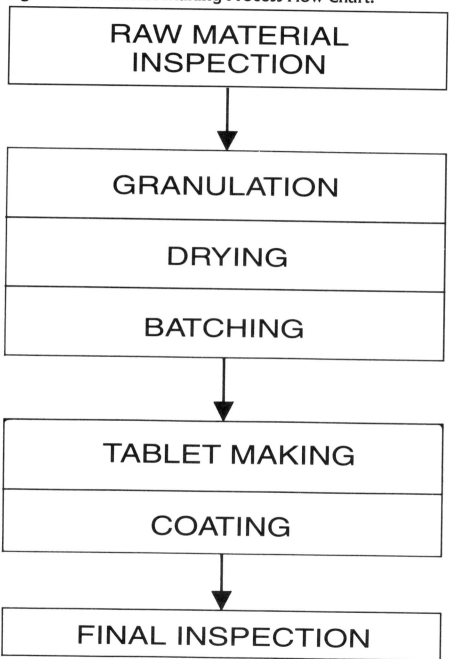

could escape solution because of unclear accountability. In this case, the manufacturing department believed that changes in raw materials and the test methods had created the problem. The department claimed to be doing all processing according to correct procedure and believed that the quality control department had not responded to a change in the raw materials. Furthermore, manufacturing believed that the quality control specifications were unrealistically tight and not indicative of the product's quality. Manufacturing also suggested that quality control develop a test that more adequately represented the product's fitness-for-use requirements. In short, manufacturing believed that problem-solving efforts should focus on the quality control department.

On the other hand, the quality control department believed the problem lay with manufacturing. Quality control was reluctant to change test methods because raw materials had not changed a great deal and manufacturing previously had been able to make acceptable product. Another reason for their reluctance was that they felt the product with a longer disintegration time was substantially different from the product with the shorter disintegration time and could be considered a different product. If this were true, the government regulatory bodies could intervene because the company would be marketing a different product without approval. However, quality control admitted that there may have been a subtle change in the raw materials. A similar problem with disintegration had occurred about a year earlier and had been resolved after the vendor claimed to have changed his drying technique. Because the problems appeared to be similar and changes in raw materials were on both the manufacturing and quality control list of possible causes, both departments agreed to have an in-house task force concentrate its investigation on raw material changes.

Tasks were assigned to both the manufacturing and quality control departments that focused on the raw materials problem but also looked into improved testing methods. The manufacturing department began an intensive effort to establish a better relationship with the vendor to see what could be done about improving the raw materials. Furthermore, manufacturing tried developing a use test to screen incoming raw material. This test involved making small batches of the final product in order to differentiate satisfactory from unsatisfactory raw material.

The quality control department concentrated on intensive analysis of all the accumulated data and contracted with outside laboratories to develop new raw material tests. In addition, quality control developed the criteria for easier release tests and was also prepared to do actual user tests to qualify product. However, after several months, the problem was still not resolved. Therefore, management agreed to have an outside team assist the problem-solving efforts.

Quantification

Existing records of the problem usually indicated only how many batches were rejected. In some cases, however, the records also included how many of the six tablets in a sample failed to disintegrate in the required time and stated the time it took for the last tablet to disintegrate. The problem-solving team plotted these results on control charts to examine trends. From these plots, it became obvious that the measurement technique was inadequate for the purposes of detecting subtle changes in the product. A more sensitive scale for the product was needed—one that could detect when relative results, not simply rejects or acceptables, were being obtained. *Pass* testing only allows a decision of *pass* or *fail* and does not provide data that can be analyzed in any detail.

To begin, the team recorded the disintegration times for each tablet separately. Previously, when a batch had failed, it was not clear from the data whether it failed because the average disintegration time of the batch was increasing, whether the spread of the values was increasing, or whether there were occasional outliers. The team proposed a more meaningful test—one that would be time consuming, often requiring an analyst to observe and record data for over half an hour. This test would also require more than six tablets per testing batch—30 or more tablets were chosen as a suitable sample size for obtaining data. It was not obvious how many batches would have to be tested or how much useful data the test would produce. However, pressures to resolve the problem helped the team find an automated test apparatus and testing began.

The Multi-Vari Study

Assumption of a wide normal curve of disintegration time extending beyond the cutoff point of 30 minutes as indicated in Figure 19-2 was shown to be incorrect. It was, in fact, found that there were two distributions of disintegration times. The result was a bimodal distribution as shown in Figure 19-3. In some batches all tablets were acceptable and in all rejected batches most tablets were acceptable, meaning that regardless of raw material changes it was possible to make good tablets from all materials. Thus, the new raw material could not be the only cause of the problem. This observation proved critical and changed the nature of the investigation. The issue became one of discovering what factor in the process caused some tablets to go bad.

Samples were taken to identify where the variation was greatest. The main types of variation were found to be time-

Figure 19-2. Assumed Distribution of Disintegration Times.

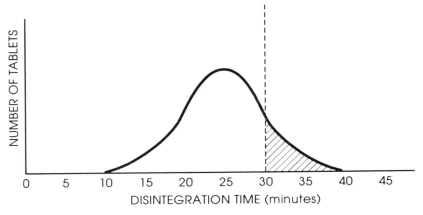

Figure 19-3. Actual Distribution of Disintegration Times.

to-time and place-to-place. Time-to-time variation appeared as differences between consecutive batches made from the same raw materials. Place-to-place variation involved the difference between product made in the laboratory and product made in the factory. All tablets made in the laboratory passed the test and some batches made in the factory passed, but some batches made in the factory exhibited the bimodal distribution of disintegration times as shown in Figure 19-3.

A bimodal distribution of results indicates that there is within-batch variation. In the past, the granulation process had been identified as a source of within-batch variation because there seemed to be considerable leeway in the operating procedures. The team now intended to focus its attention on that process; however, the study found nothing to indicate problems before or after the tablet-making process, which takes place after granulation. Therefore, the problem had to arise after that point.

The only process after tablet making was the coating process. The first product deviation from specification occurred after the coating. It was observed that tablets coated just before employees' break time did not exhibit excessive disintegration times. Multi-vari tests were then performed on the coating process. Samples were taken immediately after the coating started, in the middle of the coating operation, and at the end of the coating operation. The study revealed that if tablets were ultimately rejected, the problem occurred within the first two minutes of the start of the coating operation. If no rejectable tablets were produced during the first two minutes, there would be no rejectable tablets. Since the only part of the coating process that occurred in the first two minutes was the heatup of the equipment, this was a strong indication that the problem of rejectable tablets was heat (temperature) related.

During the coating process, the tablets were placed on a three-layer rotating drum, then heated, rotated, and coated. The coater used for this product had a variable speed gear for rotating the drum—a low speed for heatup and a high speed for coating. However, the low-speed gear needed repair and required an operator to make a screwdriver adjustment at the back of the machine to enable the drum to rotate during heatup. Since the operating instructions ignored this matter, the operator often chose not to run the drum during heatup, but ran it only at high speed after the coating operation started.

The multi-vari study tested samples from the top, middle, and bottom layers of the drum and found significant differences. The bottom and middle layers always produced good tablets, while the top layer sometimes contained rejects. Because the operators did not always rotate the drum during heatup, the tablets in the top layers often overheated and then failed to pass the tests. The immediate solution was to start the rotation and heating simultaneously. In addition, the mystery of "no rejects just before break time" was solved—just before break the operator did not leave the tablets in the drum long enough to overheat.

The Designed Experiment

With the knowledge it accumulated, the team designed an experiment to test the effects of time and temperature. In this experiment, tablets were heated in an oven to determine the effects of heat on the coating process. Figure 19-4 depicts the results. As the temperature to which the tablets were heated increased, the average disintegration time (and variation) increased considerably, particularly above a critical temperature.

Figure 19-4. Distributions of Disintegration Times of Batches Being Tested at Various Temperatures.

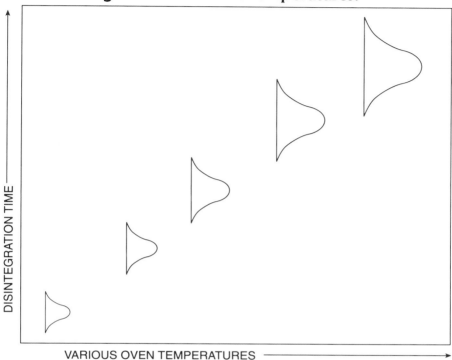

This critical temperature was the melting point of one of the lubricants used in the process. Replacement of this lubricant by one of a higher melting point could reduce the effect of the lubricant on the disintegration times.

A question still existed about changes in the raw material. Using a temperature versus disintegration time scale, the team now had a means of differentiating "good" material from "bad." The team found that the "good" material was crystalline and less heat sensitive while the "bad" material was amorphous and heat sensitive. However, all good tablets could be made from the so-called bad material if they were carefully heated and treated.

The cause of the problem turned out to be a three-factor interaction involving the new amorphous raw material, the lubricant, and the method of operation of the coating process.

All three factors had to be present simultaneously to produce rejectable tablets. The problem could be solved by avoiding the new amorphous material, using a lubricant that was not so heat sensitive, and/or maintaining a close watch during the coating operation to avoid overheating the top layer. The permanent solution was to change to a less heat-sensitive lubricant. A remaining issue, however, was why the operators were allowed discretion as to whether to rotate the drum during the heatup cycle. The team found that the gear had broken about a year previously and the crystalline raw material then being used, which was not so heat sensitive, could make good tablets whether or not the drum was rotated during heatup. Therefore, rotating the drum during the heatup cycle was not considered important and was often ignored.

The Case of Nondisintegrating Tablets

Step 1—Provide focus. There were many batches that failed the USP test requirements so they had to be scrapped. Also, there were some customer complaints that the tablets did not disintegrate.

Step 2—Get close to the problem. The outside team was shown all the process steps.

Step 3—Quantify the output. The existing test was a prescribed pass-fail test. A major breakthrough came when the team developed a test procedure to provide good variables data.

Step 4—Run multi-vari study(ies). Multi-vari data were collected on piece-to-piece (tablet-to-tablet) (within batch), time-to-time (batch-to-batch), and place-to-place (between laboratory and factory). Multi-vari studies were run on step-to-step in the process and then layer-to-layer in the drum used during coating.

Step 5—Design experiment(s). The multi-vari study solved the manufacturing problem but did not explain *why* the phenomenon worked. The designed experiment explained the mystery of *why*. A three-factor interaction existed and all three factors had to be present simultaneously to cause the problem.

Step 6—Turn the problem on and off. The team turned the problem on and off by changing any one of the three interacting variables.

Step 7—Optimize. Once the problem was understood, optimizing was not required.

Step 8—Install process controls on key variable(s). A change in any one of the three interacting variables controlled the process.

Step 9—Measure before and after results. Before the study, management considered dropping a multimillion-dollar product and after the study the problem was eliminated and the product line saved.

Chapter 20

The Case of the Eccentric Discs

A large manufacturer was punching a disc from a flexible material using a punch press with progressive punches/dies. There were a number of discs across the web with the first set of punches removing the center hole and then locating from this hole to punch the disc from the web. There was a concentricity requirement between the center hole and the outside diameter. If the disc did not meet the concentricity requirement there would be an unacceptable vibration when the disc rotated in use.

Discs that did not meet the concentricity requirement were rejected in the plant when they were found. The cost of 100% inspection was prohibitive, so many discs that did not meet the concentricity requirement found their way into customer applications. In addition, there was a multimillion-dollar market opportunity awaiting these discs if the concentricity could be controlled to less than half of the present specification. Measurement of concentricity or eccentricity was accomplished by placing the disc over a hub on a fixture and rotating the disc. An indicator against the outside of the disc read the amount of eccentricity.

The operator was one of the most conscientious and hardworking people in the plant. Whenever he found that eccentricity was higher than allowed he would start making adjustments to the punch press and/or ancillary feed equipment. He realized that the most eccentric discs were produced on the edge cavities. He also noted that if the left disc eccentricity was getting much too high, he could adjust it down, but then the disc cut in the right cavity would tend to get worse. As he successfully brought the left disc into specification, the right cavity would begin to produce marginal and rejectable discs. In fact, he kept the discs separated by cavity so that if the left disc was getting too eccentric he could scrap just those discs, knowing that the center and right discs would be mostly acceptable. On occasion, an edge cavity would produce discs so far out of specification that the adjacent cavity would also produce some discs out of specification.

Production management considered not using the left and right side punches (cavities), but that would cause a significant loss of capacity as well as waste the material on the edges of the web (roll). Also, someone recommended replacing the punch press, which had progressive punches/dies, and buying a punch press that cut the center hole and outside at once. This action would have been very costly and time consuming.

The corporate engineering office was brought in to see if it could resolve the dilemma. The engineers used the traditional four-step engineering approach of *Observe, Think, Try*, and *Explain*. They *observed* the machine, ancillary feed equipment, material, and operator in action; took notes; and returned to their offices for a brainstorming session to *think* of what the problem might be. They made several recommendations that they could implement (*try*). Their recommendations fell into five general categories and totaled 15 individual actions. The cost of implementing the changes relating to the punch press alone approached $200,000. There were recommendations for changing procedures to better control the incoming rolls of material, changes in the inspection procedure to remove some of the alleged raw material problems, and recommendations for monitoring and maintaining the punch press replacement parts as well as changes in inspection procedures of the finished discs. Hopefully these corrective actions would solve the problem so they could *explain* what had caused the problem.

Between the time of their review of the problem and the recommendations for its correction, an industrial investigator was assigned to work on the problem. Quantification is the first diagnostic step and there already existed a fixture for measuring eccentricity. However, a reading of eccentricity does not fully explain within-piece variation, so the first innovation was to plot the results of the eccentricity reading at 12 points around the circumference of the disc (a clock diagram; see Figure 20-1). Three consecutive discs are plotted on Figure 20-1.

A multi-vari study was run, taking five consecutive discs several times from each of the cavities and looking at the eccentricity at 12 points around the disc in relation to the disc's orientation as it traveled through the punch press. In Figure 20-1, three consecutive discs are plotted. If there had been no eccentricity all plots would have been on the zero axis (the dotted line) in the clock diagram.

The investigators found very little time-to-time variation and very little disc-to-disc (piece-to-piece) variation. The

Figure 20-1. Eccentricity.

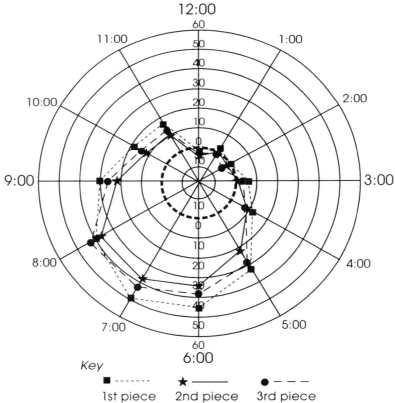

within-piece variation is the eccentricity, but the exciting result was that the eccentricity was oriented the same way, that is, the thinnest and thickest areas were always in the same location in relation to how the web of material went through the machine. Again see Figure 20-1, which shows how consistent the orientation of the eccentricity was from disc-to-disc. The investigators then adjusted the machine and found they could shift the eccentricity across the web, but the *orientation* of the thinnest/thickest areas did not change. The machine could not be adjusted to make all good discs. It was not presently capable of meeting tolerances. The investigators wondered if the punches/dies were out of specification. They then sent a rigid material (an aluminum sheet) through the punch press and measured the eccentricity of all the discs and found that all discs across the web had extremely good concentricity. The punches/dies did a fine job if the material was rigid. The flexible material was being shifted between the two stations in the press, and the further away from the center, the more the distortion. No wonder the operator worked so hard—he had an impossible task.

A clever engineer found a neat way of holding down the edge of the material between the two steps of the punching operation so it could not be pulled inward from the edges during punching. The fix was under $6,000. The eccentricity of the discs after this fix was installed not only met the specification all the time but also was small enough to allow entry into a previously untapped multimillion-dollar market.

Once again, the more detailed look into within-piece measurement (i.e., orientation of the eccentricity in relation to the web going through the punch press), coupled with meaningful plotting of the data (clock diagrams), proved to be the key to solving a previously mysterious problem.

The Case of the Eccentric Discs

Step 1—Provide focus. There was a high in-plant scrap rate, numerous customer complaints, and a market not accessible because of high eccentricity of the discs made of flexible material.

Step 2—Get close to the problem. The investigator noted that a very conscientious operator frequently adjusted the punch press and rejected many of the discs after measuring their concentricity (eccentricity).

Step 3—Quantify the output. The operator measured the amount of eccentricity by placing the disc over a hub on a fixture and rotating the disc. The investigator instituted the crucial step of recording the orientation of the disc in relation to the material going through the punch press.

Step 4—Run multi-vari study(ies). The investigator ran a multi-vari study looking at piece-to-piece, time-to-time, and cavity-to-cavity variation. Eccentricity is the within-piece variation, but the investigator also reviewed the within-piece variation considering orientation of the material going through the punch press.

Step 5—Design experiment(s). The multi-vari study solved the problem so a designed experiment was not needed.

Step 6—Turn the problem on and off. The investigator turned the problem on and off by showing the effects of eccentricity from any given cavity when he adjusted the web. By tightening or removing the hold-downs on the edges, the problem could be turned on and off.

Step 7—Optimize. By turning the problem on and off, an optimizing step was not required.

Step 8—Install process controls on key variable(s). Occasional measurements of eccentricity verified the efficacy of the solution.

Step 9—Measure before and after results. Rejects stopped, customer complaints stopped, and a new market was available.

Chapter 21

The Case of the Spline Demerits

New Process Gear of Chrysler was having trouble meeting size requirements on some of the 23 tooth-drive–gear splines for the transmission of the Dakota Truck. The company ran numerous studies over many months both on machining and on the effect that heat treating had on the size of the splines. Inevitably, the audits found undersize splines and therefore they received demerits. The spline-rolling machine was slated for a $180,000 rebuild when industrial investigators were called in. The investigators created a training program to teach four cross-functional problem-solving teams how to isolate key variables so they could apply this approach to the spline problem in addition to three other problems.

The splines had been inspected using a functional gauge, which is an excellent way to determine if a spline will work properly in a transmission. However, a functional gauge is a go/not-go gauge and is inadequate for problem solving. A numerical-scale (variable) gauge was needed. One should not confuse product-acceptance–pass testing with problem-solving testing. The team had a new gauge built that measured the pitch diameter across all 23 teeth so the investigators could see within-piece variation—that is, all 23 diameters. The gauge was evaluated using the repeatability and reproducibility test for evaluating gauges (see Bibliography, Traver, "Measuring Equipment Repeatability—The Rubber Ruler"). The gauge did not pass the R&R test because R&R equaled 31% of the tolerance. The gauge was reworked and improved and passed the R&R test quite nicely.

With the quantification issue well in hand, the investigators were ready for the multi-vari study. They measured three samples of 5 consecutive splines across all 23 diameters immediately after the spline roller. After the parts were heat treated the investigators remeasured these 15 splines across all 23 diameters.

The problem-solving teams found that the piece-to-piece (spline-to-spline) variation was very small: the spline roller repeated very well. Also they found very little difference between the three 5-spline samples (time-to-time). The teams received three surprises. There was considerable variation within the spline, that is, from tooth-to-tooth, and this within-piece pattern of variation was consistent from one spline to the next (see Figure 21-1). Spline 2 was typical.

The green tolerance (before heat treat) was 0.0009 inch and the finish-size tolerance (after heat treat) was 0.0012 inch. The variation in diameter from tooth to tooth for the green splines measured about 0.0013 inch: more than the finish-size tolerance. The third surprise was that the spline did not increase in size, due to heat treat, the expected 0.0010–0.0013 inch, but instead grew only 0.0002–0.0004 inch (see Figure

Figure 21-1. Pitch Diameters on Spline #2 Before and After Heat Treat.

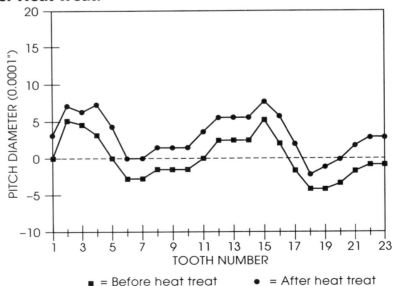

■ = Before heat treat   ● = After heat treat

21-2). In fact, this growth was extremely consistent, so the shape did not change. It had been virtually impossible to see what had been happening when the functional gauge was used to judge the parts.

The racks that form the splines were replaced with new racks for less than $6,000. With these new racks the variation in the diameters of the splines was reduced from about 0.0013 inch to less than 0.0007 inch (see Figure 21-3). The tooth-to-tooth (within-piece) pattern remained the same but the amount of out-of-round was much less. Now that the true growth due to heat treat was well documented and understood, the nominal size before heat treat was raised closer to the finished (after heat treat) size.

With the new racks and a higher nominal before heat treat, parts were run to verify the effectiveness of the two corrective actions. One hundred percent of the parts made were now comfortably within final tolerance (see Figure 21-4). The $180,000 rebuild for the spline-rolling machine was canceled and the drive-gear spline was no longer a warranty concern for New Process Gear or the customer.

Figure 21-2. Change in Pitch Diameters on Spline #2 as a Result of Heat Treat.

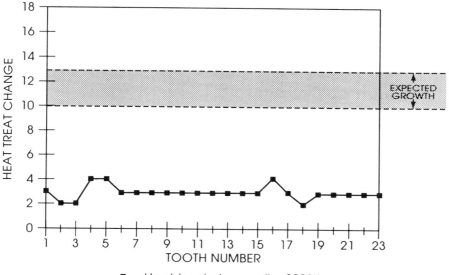

Figure 21-3. Pitch Diameters on Spline #3 with the New Racks.

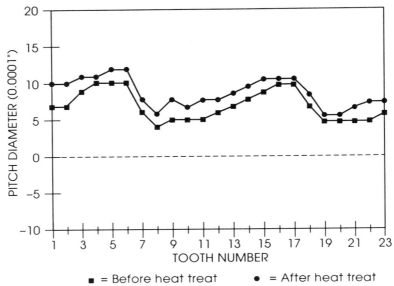

■ = Before heat treat   ● = After heat treat

Figure 21-4. Pitch Diameters on Spline #5 with the New Racks and a Higher Nominal.

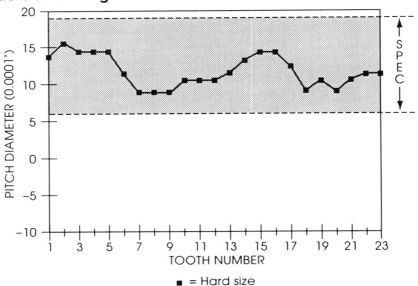

■ = Hard size

The Case of Spline Demerits

Step 1 — Provide focus. The audits always found undersize splines.

Step 2 — Get close to the problem. The cross-functional problem-solving team looked closely at the spline-rolling machine and the functional gauge used to measure the finished splines.

Step 3 — Quantify the output. A crucial step was to build a gauge that could measure the pitch diameter over all 23 teeth.

Step 4 — Run multi-vari study(ies). The team measured five consecutive splines immediately after spline rolling to look at within-piece, piece-to-piece, time-to-time, and before and after heat treatment variation.

Step 5 — Design experiment(s). The multi-vari study provided all the necessary information to solve the problem so no designed experiment was run.

Step 6 — Turn the problem on and off. Once the new racks were put in place, the incidence of undersize splines disappeared completely.

Step 7 — Optimize. Optimization was not necessary because the problem-solving team eliminated the problem.

Step 8 — Install process controls on key variable(s). The functional gauge was used to verify that all parts were functional.

Step 9 — Measure before and after results. The 23-tooth spline that had been high on the list of demerits disappeared from the list.

Chapter 22

The Case of the Mysterious Hot Crank

When a brand-new car is run until it is very hot, has the ignition turned off for a short while, and then fails to turn over fast enough to restart, the car is called a "hot crank" car. (Definitions pertinent to hot starting problems are shown in Figure 22-1.) In this situation, mechanics and service station attendants may try various solutions to fix the car. However, the effectiveness of these solutions depends primarily on how long they take. Cooling of the engine is what actually allows the car to start.

The cause of the hot crank phenomenon eluded the automotive industry for many years. As engines grew in size over the years, starters became larger and more powerful. By continually increasing the power of the starter, the hot crank situation would abate for a while. Cold weather also seemed to reduce the problem and it could be forgotten for another year. However, the hot crank problem became critical at one major automobile manufacturer during the end of 1966 production (summer of 1966). The problem was complicated by the fact that there was no more room available for a larger starter. A redesigned starting system in the same space for the 1967 model year would have cost more than a million dollars and engineering management doubted that even this system would cure the problem.

These conditions prompted the manufacturer to ask an outside problem-solving team to join the engineering department to help resolve the longstanding problem. Five weeks later the major cause of the problem had been isolated, a correction instituted, and the problem eliminated from produc-

Figure 22-1. Hot Crank Problem Terminology.

Minimum Start Speed
The minimum speed at which an engine must turn to start and sustain continuous combustion. Typically, this minimum speed is about 40 to 60 rpm.

Hot Crank
The condition where the starter will not turn a hot engine at its minimum start speed.

Startability
The engine temperature (most simply approximated by oil temperature) at which an engine goes from a moderate to a hard start. This partly subjective measure has proved to be useful in identifying differences in engines. Two engines might both be hot crank problems but a startability measure can show whether one is more of a problem than the other. Investigation of the difference in engines can lead to identification of important variables affecting startability.

Hot Start
The condition where an engine can be turned in excess of the minimum starting speed but will not start. Carburetor, fuel pump, or electrical components, for example, could be the cause of hot start problems.

tion. Over the next few months, during the second phase of the problem-solving program, the team obtained more detailed engineering information to fully understand the cause of hot crank cars. In the third phase, the team investigated additional refinements and longer-term solutions at a reduced scale of effort.

Initiation of Study

The first step taken by the problem-solving team was to become acquainted with the hot crank phenomenon by looking at production cars that failed to start at high engine temperature. The most obvious problem with testing these production cars was the existence of an attribute-type rating scale in which a car was classified either as a ''hot crank'' problem car or as a ''good'' car. This scale was inadequate. Before the problem could be solved, and, in fact, before any test could be run, it was important to establish a measuring system that could be used to assess the degree of hot crank.

Another serious problem was the lack of repeatability in

the measurement of water temperature at the upper radiator hose in relation to the incidence of hot crank. This measurement was used as an indication of engine temperature. The team, however, found that measurement of oil temperature was more repeatable and better represented the temperature inside the engine. Also, measuring oil temperature with a thermocouple at the bottom of the dipstick could be done easily.

Developing a Testing Procedure

The team proceeded to develop a test procedure, as shown in the example in Figure 22-2, in which a car was started and left to idle. A cover was then placed over the car's grill to prevent air from cooling the radiator so the temperature of the engine rose. When the oil temperature reached 201°F, the engine was shut off for one minute, and then an attempt was made to restart the engine. If the car started easily at that temperature, an E, for easy, was placed in the column labeled "Type of Start." The car was then allowed to idle until the oil temperature read 209°F. Again, the car was shut off for one minute and

Figure 22-2. Example of Test Temperatures and Results.

LOW-LIMIT STARTER—10W		
TEST NO.	OIL TEMP. (°F)	TYPE OF START E, M, H, O
1	201	E
2	209	E
3	217	M
4	225	M
5	233	H
6	241	O
7	249	
8	257	

KEY: E = EASY START, M = MODERATE START,
H = HARD START, O = NO START   STARTABILITY 229

a restart was tried. If this start also was easy, an E was placed in the 209°F oil temperature row under the "Type of Start" column.

In Figure 22-2, the 201°F and 209°F starts were both easy and the 217°F and 225°F starts were moderate (M). This car became a hard start (H) at 233°F and failed to start (O) at 241°F. The team defined a numerical figure for startability as halfway between moderate start and hard start. The car shown in Figure 22-2 was halfway between 225°F and 233°F; therefore, the car was labeled with a startability figure of 229°F—a figure that repeated well on subsequent tests. The numerical figure identified a car's startability and therefore the team could measure the effect of subsequent changes to that car's engine.

Some cars did not reach a hard start within the range tested. Therefore, a higher-pressure radiator cap was used to increase the boiling point of the engine's coolant so that the team could test above even 249°F. All subsequent hot crank testing was performed with the higher-pressure radiator caps.

Cars were "hot cranked" using this new test procedure as they came off the production line, with the team recording oil temperature and determining a figure that was labeled "startability." This startability figure could be used to compare any one or combinations of the seven variables the team decided to record for each car. These variables included 2- versus 4-barrel carburetors, air conditioning or no air conditioning, 9.9 or 10.2 compression ratio, 11- or 13-plate batteries, "Step II" (a more powerful starter) versus standard starter, battery-specific gravity of greater than 1.240 versus lower than 1.240, and 20W oil in the crankcase versus 10W oil.

During the testing, a few pairs of cars were brought to engineering that were theoretically identical, but one in each pair had a very high startability and one had a very low startability. A component search test was made on these cars while other testing was continued and the data analyzed.

Test Results

The results of the testing were as follows:

- Oil viscosity turned out to be a key variable: 20W oil in place of 10W oil raised startability about 20°F.
- The 13-plate battery was approximately 7°F better on the startability scale than the 11-plate battery.
- Batteries with a specific gravity higher than 1.240 were a few degrees better in startability than batteries in the 1.225 to 1.240 range.
- The Step II starter, which was more expensive, was not better than the standard starter.
- There was no difference between 4-barrel and 2-barrel carburetor cars.
- Air-conditioned cars were not different from non-air-conditioned cars.
- Because the data were unbalanced, the compression ratio effect could not be evaluated and had to wait for later testing.

Figure 22-3 is a plot of one of the component search investigations. The figure shows the startability of two cars, one of which had very high startability (250) and the other which had very low startability (192). This pair was selected because it

Figure 22-3. Example of Component Search Test Results.

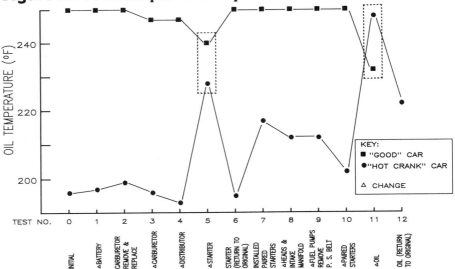

represented the extremes in startability numbers and knowledge is often in the extremes.

The team made a total of 12 exchanges on the two cars. Prior to the fifth exchange, little difference in the startability of the two cars was noted. A substantial difference, however, occurred at test 5 in which the starters were swapped. While the "good" car dropped about 10 degrees in startability, the hot crank car showed a remarkable improvement. In test 6 the starters were again exchanged and the test results returned virtually to where they were at test 4, proving that at least part of the problem involved the starters. The starter that originally was in the hot crank car was sent to the supplier for testing where it was found to have two shorted coils.

Testing continued at test 7 where two carefully matched starters were used to replace the original starters. The result was a substantial improvement in the startability of the hot crank car and virtually no change in the startability of the "good" car. This result verified the role that the starters played in hot startability. However, something else was contributing to the hot crank problem.

Little change was noticed in tests 8, 9, and 10. In test 11 the engine oils were swapped and the results were dramatic. The hot crank car became a "good" car and the "good" car's startability dropped substantially. An investigation of the oils showed that the hot crank car originally had 10W oil in the crankcase and the "good" car had 20W oil. Putting the 10W oil back into the hot crank car (test 12) substantially decreased the startability, proving that at least part of the problem could be turned on and off.

The conclusion at the end of the testing was that the low startability car had two problems: a defective starter and 10W oil in the crankcase. Replacing the defective starter corrected part of the problem and changing to 20W oil corrected the rest. The component search study also revealed that further investigation of starters and oil was required.

The Designed Experiment

Next, five hot crank problem cars (low startability figures) were tested in a two-variable designed experiment. The two variables tested were 10W and 20W oil and starters from the lower and upper ends of the specification. Testing began by starting all five cars in random order with all four combinations of oils and starters. The 20W oil resulted in about 22°F higher startability than the 10W oil (see Figure 22-4), so unquestionably 20W oil raised startability. While the high-limit starter showed only a slight improvement over the low-limit starter, a later check showed that the two starters were, in fact, nearly identical in torque, rather than substantially different, as was the case with the starters in the component search test.

The team wondered if the same results could be obtained on a "test buggy" instead of in a car and also what would happen if other oils, for example modified 10W (commercially, 10W-30), were tried. Test results were repeated when the team tested five engines on a buggy using 10W, 10W-30, and 20W-20 oils (see Figure 22-5). The 10W-30 break-in oil was considered a substitute for 20W because engines would have to be stored and then used during cold weather; 20W oil, although effective for reducing hot crank problems, would have been undesirable under cold weather conditions. Results of startability testing showed that using the 10W-30 oil resulted in an average of about 82% of the improvement that could be ob-

Figure 22-4. Results of the Designed Experiment.

		STARTER	
		LOW LIMIT	HIGH LIMIT
O I L	**10W**	215.3	221.0
	20W	241.3	239.0

Figure 22-5. Effect of Oil Type on Startability.

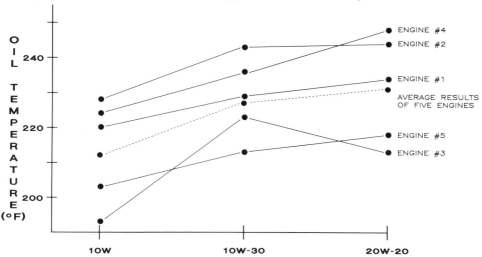

tained by using 20W versus 10W. Figure 22-5 shows the average plot of the five engines tested as well as the five individual engines.

The question of high and low compression had not been answered in the initial testing, and the effect of high- and low-limit starters had not been determined in the starter versus oil designed experiment because the "high-limit" starter was in fact not near the high limit. The effect of an advanced spark thus entered the picture. Therefore, the team ran another designed experiment, using a high- and low-limit starter and two distributors—one with a fixed spark advance of 6 degrees and one with a fixed spark advance of 13 degrees. The compression ratio was varied by using gaskets of different thickness. The resulting two compression ratios were 9.9:1 and 10.5:1.

Changing from the low-limit starter to the high-limit starter made about a 26°F difference in startability. The difference made by changing from a 9.9 to a 10.5 compression ratio was under 4°F, while the difference between the 6-degree and 13-degree advanced spark was only 1°F and thus was considered not to be significant. Advancing the spark too much would make starting more difficult, but this advance must be 20 degrees or even higher.

Dynamometer Testing

During the testing period, the team set up a dynamometer to determine engine starting torque requirements and to better understand why the solution had worked. Engines were turned at 50 rpm for testing under simulated starting conditions. The most lucrative variable for immediate investigation was oil viscosity, so the torque required to turn an engine at 50 rpm at a temperature above 200°F was compared when 10W, 10W-30, or 20W oil was in the crankcase. Figure 22-6 shows that a test engine using 10W oil required about the same starting torque as when the engine was 20 degrees hotter and had 20W oil in the crankcase. All testing thus confirmed the 20°F difference in startability between these oils. The 10W-30 again fell between the 10W and the 20W, but closer to the 20W.

In order to summarize the testing up to this point, the team developed a Pareto chart showing the main variables considered in startability and the effect or lack of effect each had on startability. This chart clearly indicated that the largest gain

Figure 22-6. Torque Required to Turn Engines at 50 rpm vs. Oil Viscosity and Engine Oil Temperature.

at the least cost involved using a heavier oil. To obtain a major increase in starter torque would be a great help, but this was a costly consideration. With the major improvement obtained from the heavier oil, the purchase of the 13-plate battery would be well out along the scale of diminishing returns.

Analyses of the Testing

The thinner oil at higher temperature lost its lubricating ability and drained from the walls of mating surfaces. If the engine were restarted immediately, the oil would not yet have drained from the walls, while a longer time period allowed for cooling contraction and thus greater clearances between mating surfaces. Hot crank was most pronounced if the engine was turned off while hot and allowed to cool only a few minutes. Torque required to turn an engine at starting speeds is a direct function of temperature (see Figure 22-6). At running speeds the mating surfaces were in a bath of oil, and the viscosity was not an important factor. Torque requirements were not affected by oil viscosity—of those oils tested—in a running engine. Thinner oil such as kerosene allowed a hot crank problem below 150°F, while 30W, 40W, and 50W oil in the crankcase pushed the startability figure progressively higher, beyond the radiator's ability not to boil over, even for the most troublesome engine tested.

During testing, the statement was often heard that hot crank disappeared after "X" miles. This occurred because the starting torque required was reduced with use, that is, the engine was broken in. However, the value of "X" depended on the extent to which the hot crank problem had existed initially. More specifically, even though the startability figure increased (improved) with use, an engine with a very low initial startability figure could be a hot crank problem after many miles.

All of the team's testing clearly indicated that the hot crank problem was not an isolated phenomenon. Rather, it was part of a continuum on which, with high enough temperatures, "thin" enough oil, tight enough fits, and/or a poor enough starting system (including a very low battery), the problem appeared. The hot crank phenomenon was really the tail of a normal curve where most of the engines produced were within the acceptable range. When the starting system did not equal the engine requirement, the engine failed to turn over fast enough to start. The testing established that the entire problem of startability might be looked upon as a balance. On one side was starter power and on the other side was engine resistance. Pumping the accelerator pedal often alleviated the problem of hot crank and got a problem car started, because as the fresh gasoline emptied into the combustion chambers, it reduced the temperature and allowed the engine to start at a lower cranking speed. The cooling reduced friction and the engine thus was easier to start.

While there was concern that the startability testing procedure was inadequate because it used a subjective evaluation of easy, moderate, and hard to define how well a car started, the degree of repeatability of the procedure proved its value. However, if a more precise measure had been developed, even smaller engine-to-engine differences could have been detected.

Before the 10W-30 oil could be specified for production use, cold-weather testing was required. The test results showed that the 10W-30 was not as good as 10W at low temperatures or as good as 20W at high temperatures.

Another previously unanswered question had been how much torque was required to turn the engine over at higher speeds with various oil types and at varying temperatures. Figure 22-7 shows that at 50 rpm the required torque was very responsive to temperature while at 500 and 1,000 rpm temperature had little or no effect on torque. An engine turning at higher speeds is in a bath of oil and the oil temperature did not have the same effect on torque requirements.

Figure 22-7 does not, however, show the effect of different oils. As seen earlier, oils made a major difference under cranking conditions at 50 rpm. The result of testing other oils at 50 rpm yielded curves parallel to the 50 rpm curve shown. At the higher rpm's, different oils did not make any appreciable difference on torque requirements. Therefore, torque require-

Figure 22-7. Torque Required to Turn Engines vs. Engine Oil Temperature at Various RPM's.

TEMPERATURE (°F)

ments at 500 and 1,000 rpm were not affected by the use of different oils.

The one remaining area to be investigated was engine-to-engine variation due to initial fits of engine components. A designed experiment was created with two variables of engine bearing clearances and piston clearances. Two engines were built for this experiment, one with tight bearing clearances and one with loose bearing clearances, and each engine had two sets of pistons built: a tight set and loose set. Testing was performed at 50 rpm.

The results of this testing are shown in Figure 22-8. Engines with tight bearings and tight pistons required much higher starting torque than engines with loose bearings and loose pistons. The results of this designed experiment indicated that startability differences could also be caused by random variation within specifications for bearing and piston fit. This conclusion reinforced the importance of controlling process variables to the center of the specification and thus reducing variation.

Figure 22-8. Torque Required to Turn Engines vs. Engine Condition and Engine Oil Temperature.

The Case of the Mysterious Hot Crank

Step 1—Provide focus. This problem had become critical and dealers in the hot desert states were refusing shipments of new cars. The problem had reached a panic condition.

Step 2—Get close to the problem. The outside problem-solving team joined with the operations engineers to take a close look at the situation.

Step 3 — Quantify the output. A crucial step in the investigation was developing a repeatable measure on the degree of hot crank on any given car. This investigation could not proceed nor could any tests be run until this step was successfully completed.

Step 4 — Run multi-vari study(ies). Seven variables were selected for investigation so a multi-vari study was not run.

Step 5 — Design experiment(s). A number of designed experiments were run on these seven variables, usually three variables at a time. When a very high startability car and a very low startability car were obtained, a component search study was run on these two cars.

Step 6 — Turn the problem on and off. A component search investigation has "turn the problem on and off" built into its strategy. It was this "turn the problem on and off" part of the component search program that convinced management that the investigators did indeed have the answer to the problem and could demonstrate it to anyone who wished to see it.

Step 7 — Optimize. To understand why the answer worked, several optimizing studies were run to better understand how each of the variables in the three-factor interactions impacted the results.

Step 8 — Install process controls on key variable(s). Process control was implemented by specifying the correct conditions to eliminate hot crank.

Step 9 — Measure before and after results. Before the team started a panic situation existed and at the end of the study the problem was solved and the phenomenon was understood.

Chapter 23

Variables Search

Variables search is a statistically based problem-solving strategy developed by Dorian Shainin. Like multi-vari, variables search is a rough screening test that directs investigation into important areas and eliminates unimportant ones. Before a variables search test is run, engineering judgment and manufacturing experience are used to determine which variables are likely to be causing the problem being evaluated, and these variables are listed in decreasing order of importance. (This technique differs from a pure multi-vari investigation where generally no assumption is made about potential key variables before the investigation is begun.) Then, for each variable, the investigator will decide which level of the variable is likely to give a "good" result and which level will give a "bad" result.

Before running a variables search test, the investigator randomizes factors such as test order, inspection order, and raw materials that could affect the results. The investigator performs the first test with all the listed variables at the expected "good" levels and then a matching run with all the variables at their expected "bad" levels. These two tests are then run again to ensure that there is good repeatability. If the tests do not repeat well, there may be other important variables at work.

The next step in variables search is to run a pair of tests, the first of which has all variables at the "good" level, *except* the variable at the top of the list (i.e., the variable most likely to be a key variable), which is set at the "bad" level. A complementary test is run with every variable set at the "bad" level, except the top variable, which is set at the "good" level.

The investigator then proceeds to exchange variable levels

174

one at a time. This process of exchanging variable levels down the list proceeds until all the important changes have been made, that is, the original differences between the sets of results have been switched from one column to the other. Then the investigator returns to the original all "good" and all "bad" levels and repeats the tests to ensure that other unknown factors have not changed during the time the tests were run.

Manufacturing know-how and engineering judgment are important parts of the variables search strategy. From a purely statistical standpoint, variables search and multi-vari are not as "clean" as some other statistical experiments, but they work well in the hands of competent practitioners. Criticism of multi-vari and variables search generally ignores the advantages of manufacturing and engineering expertise and common sense as adjuncts to purely statistical concepts.

The Case of High Scrap Rate on an Injection-Molded Product

A problem-solving team had been asked to work on an injection-molded product that had a high scrap rate. This scrap rate, when combined with high material cost, resulted in significant losses. The scrap rate over an eight-month period was about 15%, with 3.6% being attributed to a defect called voids and 5.8% attributed to a defect called surface splay. The remaining 5.6% was due to miscellaneous defects and the result of process startup. (Startup rejects are inherent in the injection-molding process during the period before the machine reaches its "equilibrium.")

The team developed a 0 to 5 scale for both voids and splay. With a good measurement scale in hand, the team ran a multi-vari study. Where the variables for controlling a process are not clearly understood, a multi-vari study provides a good way of reducing the number of variables that must be tested. In the injection-molding process, 20 or more variables may be responsible for causing the problem. To set up a designed experiment with this many variables can be complicated and may not be successful. The multi-vari investigation in this case showed that the major type of variation for both voids and splay was time to time or run to run.

Correcting the Problem of Voids

A creative brainstorming session was held by engineering, quality assurance, and manufacturing to determine which process variables might be responsible for the voids. Based on engineering judgment, experience, and educated guessing, 11 suspected variables that fit the clues from the multi-vari study were chosen to be investigated. If 11 variables, all at two levels, had been put into a full factorial designed experiment, there would have been 2,048 conditions to be tested. Traditional fractional factorials, Taguchi methodology, and random/multiple balance test designs also were considered but were rejected as impractical because of the large number of test runs and/or problems in running the required combination of variables.

Finally, variables search was chosen as the most practical experiment that could next be run and still be statistically sound. The team wanted to know if the most important variables were actually on the list of 11 suspected variables—the variables search strategy is an efficient way of making this determination. Once the variables search strategy was selected, the brainstorming group decided what the order of importance of the 11 selected variables should be and which level of each variable would give a "good" or "bad" result. This ordering is required to use the variables search strategy most effectively.

The level of each variable that was believed would give a "good" result was listed in one column of a table and the level that was believed would give a "bad" result was listed in another column. For example, it was judged that an injection time of 7.75 seconds was better than an injection time of 6.50 seconds; a hold pressure of 1,700 psi was better than 1,300 psi; and a hold time of 6.0 seconds was better than 3.5 seconds. The list of the variables began as follows:

Variable	Good	Bad
Injection Time (sec.)	7.75	6.50
Hold Pressure (psi)	1700	1300
Hold Time (sec.)	6.0	3.5
•	•	•
•	•	•
•	•	•
•	•	•

This list continued until all 11 variables were evaluated. The first test run was with all the variables at the "good" level. The second run was with all the variables at the "bad" level. It is necessary to repeat the original conditions to ensure that other potentially important variables did not change during the test. Testing then continued by changing each variable level, one variable at a time, in the order shown on the list.

By the time the first five variables were tested, three variables were found to have an influence. A capping run with these three variables all set at their "good" levels was run and defects for voids were drastically reduced. Now these three variables were set at their "bad" levels and there were many voids. The investigators could now turn the problem on and off. These two last tests were rerun and the results were repeated. All testing including these four capping runs required only 23 tests. The total score for voids using the numerical rating scale was plotted in Figure 23-1 for these three key variables. For instance, the total defect score for voids when the hold time was 3.5 seconds was 950 points higher than when the hold time was 6.0 seconds. When the hold pressure was 1,300 psi the defect score was 866 points higher than when the hold pressure was 1,700 psi, and an injection time of 6.50 seconds caused a defect score 656 points higher than when the injection time was 7.75 seconds. Of the 11 variables tested, these three variables stood out as the top three and explained the difference between good and bad product.

When many variables are selected for testing, it is a strong indication that the most important variables are not well un-

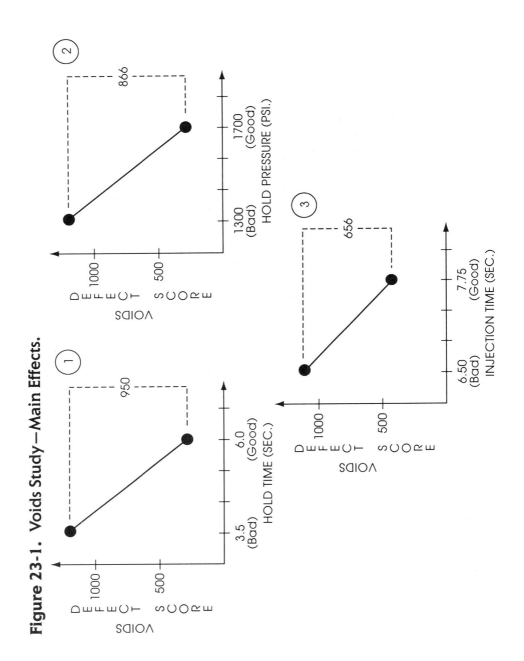

Figure 23-1. Voids Study—Main Effects.

derstood. In this case, however, the brainstorming group did very well because the three key variables were in the top five on the original list.

Once the most important variables are determined, the next step should be to analyze these variables in a full factorial designed experiment. In this case, when the three variables had been determined, a two-level matrix of these three variables was drawn. This matrix had eight (2^3) test combinations, or blocks. With the 23 runs there was already at least one test result in each of the eight blocks. When more than one number appeared in a block, the multiple results were averaged and this average was used as though it were a single test result. A standard statistical analysis (ANOVA) was made from the existing test results to further verify the relative importance of the three variables and to look for any existing interactions. If there had been any missing blocks, those blocks could have been tested and the results added to the matrix to permit statistical analysis.

Variables search is an efficient rough screening test, and, when the results are properly analyzed in a full factorial format of the key variables, it combines test efficiency with statistical assurance. When the process was run at the correct conditions determined from the study, voids were essentially nonexistent. When they did occur, the causes and corrective actions needed were obvious.

Correcting the Problem of Splay

The other major cause of scrap was splay. However, the frequency with which splay occurred suggested that optimum conditions for reducing voids would not reduce splay. This was not a surprise to the engineers because voids and splay did not necessarily occur together. A separate study was required to determine the causes of splay. After another brainstorming session, five variables were suggested as the possible culprits. With only five variables, a classical fractional factorial experiment would have been appropriate. However, the variables search strategy was chosen because of the success with the voids study, the low number of tests required, the limited availability of machine and mold time, and the company engineers' confidence and enthusiasm regarding the method. After 12 test runs the top three variables in order of importance were determined and process corrections were made.

After the completion of the studies, the process was run at the conditions testing had determined would produce the optimum results, and the scrap rates for voids and splay were a combined total of 0.1%. This figure compared to 9.4% (3.6% for voids and 5.8% for splay) for the previous eight months: a 99% reduction in scrap for these two defects. In addition, the miscellaneous and startup reject rate was reduced from 5.6% to 2%. When the major causes of defects are resolved, the frequency of defects due to other causes often is reduced because of the ability to detect and correct them more easily.

There were also some interesting side benefits to the solution of these two problems. When the problem-solving team had originally planned a program for the company there were two major aspects: equipment upgrading and statistical studies. Because of the success of the statistical studies in reducing scrap, equipment upgrading was no longer a major consideration, thus saving the company more money.

The Case of Low Pull Strength on an Electronic Component

A company's electronic component had been experiencing failures during an important quality check called a pull test. Because the component had been made using a complex manufacturing process, many variables were involved, and thus a problem-solving team determined that the variables search strategy was appropriate.

Thirteen variables were selected, placed in order of importance, and the "good/bad" levels assigned by the key technical people involved in the engineering and manufacturing of the product. The first four test runs were made in the following order: all "good," all "bad," all "bad," and all "good." The consistency between the results of the two "good" runs and also between the two "bad" runs was excellent. However, the startling observation was that the results at the all "good" level and the results at the all "bad" level were essentially identical. This meant that the problem-solving team had selected 13 variables that had no measurable effect on the pull test results. The team then went "back to the drawing board"—actually, back to the assembly area—and studied the assembly process more closely.

Subsequent investigation showed that the most important variables were related to assembly procedures that had not been considered on the list of the top 13. The variables search study had told the team that none of the listed variables was important. Any other test design, such as Taguchi methodology, classical fractional factorials, or random/multiple balance, would have required many tests and in the end the conclusion would have been that the important variables were "none of the above." The team learned this fact in four runs. The engineers had been trying to tell the process what was wrong, but with the variables search study they were able to listen to the process. Usually, the all "good" run gives a much better result than the all "bad" run and tells the investigator that the important variables are indeed on the list.

Variables Search

Step 1—Provide focus. The product selected for the study was a major concern for one of the biggest customers. The 15% total scrap rate was a real problem. "Voids" and "surface splay" totalled 9.4%.

Step 2—Get close to the problem. The problem-solving team reviewed the injection-molding operation and the inspection process.

Step 3—Quantify the output. The two top causes of scrap were voids and surface splay; both visual defects. The team developed a zero to five scale for each of the two defects.

Step 4—Run multi-vari study(ies). With the variable scale available the team ran a multi-vari study and found the pattern of variation for both defects was time-to-time or run-to-run. For voids, eleven variables fit this clue and five variables fit the clue for surface splay.

Step 5 – Design experiment(s). With such a large number of variables (11) fitting the pattern for voids the team selected a variables search designed experiment and found the top three variables. Because of the success with voids the team chose a variables search design for the five variables for surface splay.

Step 6 – Turn the problem on and off. After isolating the key variables the team ran capping runs to turn the problem on and off and demonstrated this to show management they had solved the problem.

Step 7 – Optimize. Because there was a 99% reduction in scrap the team felt they had optimized the process.

Step 8 – Install process controls on key variable(s). The new operating levels for the key variables were placed on the process. The team felt the new specifications were adequate process controls.

Step 9 – Measure before and after results. Before the study the scrap rate for voids and splay was 9.4% and was 0.1% after the study, a 99% improvement.

Chapter 24

Parallel Path Experimentation

Parallel path experimentation is a specialized form of component search or variables search. Like these techniques, parallel path is an important key variable isolation procedure because it narrows the area of investigation and moves rapidly toward identifying the cause of a problem. In component search, investigators switch parts of a product or machine to see whether a given problem changes with the changed part or stays with the unchanged parts of the product or machine. In variables search, investigators switch settings of a variable between "good" and "bad" levels to see if the problem stays with the unchanged set of variables or switches with the changed variable.

Parallel path experimentation is used when there are two (or more) production lines in a manufacturing process, each of which is producing a different quality of the same product. When one line is producing more defective product than another line, obviously something different is happening on each line. The parallel path experimentation approach attempts to locate the "bad" point in the line by sending products part of the way down one line, for example the "bad" line, and then switching the product so that it completes the rest of the process in the "good" line. Simultaneously, products sent down the "good" line are switched at the same point to finish in the "bad" line. The question then becomes what will happen: Will the "good" line become the "bad" line and the "bad" line become the "good" line, or will nothing change at all?

As an example, suppose the product going down line A

is coming out very good and the product going down line B is coming out with many defects. Because the results are noticed at the end of the line, the investigator must begin at the end of the line and work backward to find the defect-producing step.

Suppose the investigator exchanged the material going into the tenth step and found that the "good" line was now producing "bad" material and the "bad" line was now producing "good" material. This would assure that whatever was causing "badness" occurred before the tenth step in line B. The material's "badness" or "goodness" was determined before it got to the tenth step. The investigator would now move further back into the line to an earlier step, for example, the fifth step. If once again the "bad" line produced "good" material and the "good" line produced "bad" material, the defect-causing step would be before the fifth step.

If the investigator now exchanged the material going to the third step and found that the "good" line stayed "good" and the "bad" line stayed "bad," the defect-causing step would be between the third step and the fifth step. The investigator would now exchange material going to the fourth step to see if the third or fourth step was at fault. If the "good" line now produced "good" material and the "bad" line produced "bad" material, the investigator would have isolated the problem to the fourth step. Regardless of the flow of material, whatever product went through the "bad" step 4 would come out "bad" and whatever product went through the "good" step 4 would come out "good." The investigator can now turn the problem on and off.

The Case of the High Losses
of Semiconductor Chips

The following case demonstrates how parallel path experimentation was used to solve the problem experienced by a hi-tech manufacturer of semiconductor chips. At this company, production line 2 produced very "good" product, while production line 5 produced many defective products (see Figure 24-1). Using the traditional approach of Observe, Think, Try,

Figure 24-1. Semiconductor Production Line Sequence.

CURRENT SEMI-CONDUCTOR PROCESSING

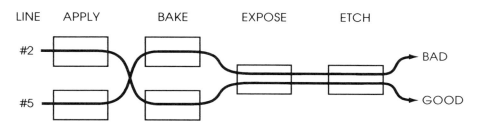

SWITCHED SEMICONDUCTOR PROCESSING

and Explain, company engineers reasoned that the variables most likely causing the problem in production line 5 were the nitrogen flow, the temperature, or the time in the bake operation. They experimented with these three variables one at a time: the traditional engineering approach, without success. Then they conducted a designed experiment with different levels of nitrogen flow and various temperatures and times, within the specifications. Regardless of the different levels tested of the three variables, problems still occurred.

Management then asked a problem-solving team to work with the engineers to correct the problem and the team suggested conducting a parallel path investigation. During this investigation, the team decided to try the first switch after the "apply" step, so at that point the product on line 2 was moved to line 5 and the product on line 5 was moved to line 2. The team found that all the chips that had gone through the apply step on line 2 and then were baked on line 5 were good. In addition, the team found that some of the chips that had gone through the apply step on line 5 and then were baked on line 2 were defective. In other words, whether the product would be good or bad was not affected by the bake operation of either line 2 or line 5. However, the apply step in line 2 always produced good product and the apply step in line 5 always produced some bad product. The problem, therefore, did not lie with the bake step, as was previously thought, but with a prior step. A subsequent switch made before the apply step did not alter the original test results, so the team concluded that the line 5 apply step was the key variable. As in the game of Twenty Questions, the team had narrowed down the problem to the line 5 apply step. Any experiments on the bake step were bound to fail because that was not the location of the problem. Once the engineers knew the source of the defects, they were able to pinpoint the problem and quickly correct it.

Parallel Path Experimentation

Step 1—Provide focus. A manufacturer had a serious problem with one of its two semiconductor processing lines.

Step 2—Get close to the problem. A problem-solving team took a close look at the multi-step process.

Step 3—Quantify the output. A good measure already existed.

Step 4—Run multi-vari study(ies). The key pattern of variation was a difference between two lines so a multi-vari study was not needed.

Step 5—Design experiment(s). The parallel path experimentation strategy is the designed experiment.

Step 6—Turn the problem on and off. By switching the product between the lines the problem could be easily turned on and off. Turning the problem on and off is built into the parallel path experimentation strategy.

Step 7—Optimize. The problem was turned on and off so the optimization step was not required.

Step 8—Install process controls on key variable(s). The engineers corrected the problem so it did not recur. Therefore, no specific process controls were needed.

Step 9—Measure before and after results. A serious problem existed before the study and after the study it no longer existed.

Epilogue

In more than half of the case histories, an essential step in isolating the key variable was developing a numerical rating scale where none existed previously. In some cases, creating a numerical rating scale was possibly the most creative part of the entire problem-solving endeavor.

In a number of the case histories, the cause of the problem was laid at the feet of the vendor, or the vendor was considered to be a part of the problem. Only in Chapter 17 was vendor material a significant factor in the cause of the problem. In Chapter 8, one of the two vendors had already been notified not to send any more material. However, the actual cause of the problem was not related to the raw material. Blaming the vendor often gets the technical people temporarily off the hook, and they do not seek the real causes.

It is interesting to note that in none of the case histories was the problem caused by the operator. It is true that operators can cause isolated sporadic incidents because of some error or mistake, but chronic problems such as those described in the case histories are almost always caused by problems with the system, an unknown variable(s), or an interaction of two or more variables. Management and supervision often blame the operator and suggest apathy, neglect, or outright carelessness. Our experience shows that operators almost always want to do a quality job. The desire for quality seems to be inherent in human beings. Management needs to harness this natural desire. Blaming the operator seems to be a simple "out" that tends to obscure the real cause.

In many companies, Statistical Process Control (SPC) methods have been looked upon as the solution to quality problems. Therefore, SPC tools such as $\overline{X}$ bar and R charts, precontrol, or other charts have been installed. These tools are primarily to hold the gains already made and they do not consider within-piece variation. In 6 of the 21 case histories in this book, the major pattern of variation was within-piece, and we were able to solve these problems because we looked at within-piece variation.

Managers of American industries seem quite willing to spend large sums of money on capital improvements to solve problems of product variability. However, in many of the case histories, the large sums of money about to be appropriated would have done little if anything to solve the problem; the delay in getting the capital expenditure into place would have taken the spotlight off the problem, and no one would have investigated the real causes of the problem. When you think that the new equipment is going to solve the problem, everyone simply waits for its arrival and installation.

APPENDIXES

Multi-Vari Exercises

The basic concept of multi-vari is straightforward. When a person faces a real-life problem, however, what to do is not always so obvious. Reading the preceding chapters of this book will provide the reader with a foundation of knowledge, but the true value of the book lies in the application of that knowledge to those real-life problems.

An excellent way of learning what to do is by evaluating either real-life experiences or "synthetic" examples. In the following exercises, the words that describe the problem are realistic but hypothetical data were used so several solutions to the same problem could be used for class exercises. These exercises should assist the reader in learning how to apply multi-vari analysis.

Appendix I

Rope Consistency

The Process

Making polyester rope is a chemical-mechanical process. Various chemicals are mixed at controlled concentrations, pressures, and temperatures to form a tankful of syrupy liquid plastic; the plastic syrup is then left to age in the tank for 24 hours under controlled conditions.

After aging, the syrup is squirted through hundreds of nozzles (a device called a spinnerette) into a chemical bath which, on contact, transforms the syrupy streams into solid streams, each of which becomes a filament or thread that will become part of a polyester rope. The rope is continually withdrawn from the bath at a controlled rate by a spinning line—a long train of wheels, some driven, some idling, that spin the threads or filaments into rope through a succession of rinsing, drying, and conditioning stations. Driving wheel speeds, idler wheel torques, rinsing, drying, and conditioning temperatures and times are some of the variables that can be adjusted to change the characteristics of the final product.

While the filaments are still partially plastic, controlled tension is applied to the rope to draw the individual fibers down to the desired diameter. The process is continuous, 24 hours a day, seven days a week, with shifts changing at 8 A.M., 4 P.M., and midnight. Several tanks are used—while one tankful is being fed to the spinning line (a process of about 6 hours) other tanks are in various stages of aging.

The Problem

Control of rope weight per meter of length is important and weight is measured routinely at the end of the process by weighing, in grams, a 10-meter sample. The rope weight varies somewhat, but the loss due to excessive variation has become substantial in this company. The task is to seek possible causes for this excessive variation.

Although many process variables are known to have an influence on rope weight, the question is which one (or more) of the variables (the *key* variable or variables) is likely to be causing the major portion of the variation observed in the end product.

The suspected variables include:

- Purity of any of six raw materials—some bought in small lot quantities, some in barge-loads. Each raw material has multiple suppliers.
- Precision of controls during mixing—such as rate of agitation, temperatures, quantities added, duration of agitation, cleanliness of tanks.
- Controls during aging—such as time, temperature, pressure, viscosity.
- Spinnerette malfunctions—plugged or partially plugged holes, extrusion pressure, viscosity.
- Coagulation bath variables—bath temperature, concentration, flow patterns.
- Postbath variables—tension applied while plastic, rate of release of tension, speed of withdrawal, temperatures at the various stages, slippages on withdrawing wheels.
- Measurement errors—sample length, scale accuracy and repeatability, moisture content of sample.

Your task is to find out which one (or more) of the numerous possible causes is primarily responsible for the variation in the weight of the final product. The approach is to look for patterns of variation. You are not expected to be able to pinpoint individual variables.

The Strategy of the Study

The objective of the synthetic example is to narrow the field of suspected causes: to be able to answer the question, "Is it animal, vegetable, or mineral?" and then to further define the animal, vegetable, or mineral.

The multi-vari study should rule out many "pet" theories and guesses and either bring to light a solution or reduce the remaining possibilities so that any subsequent designed experiments would have a very high likelihood of isolating the key variable(s).

The Multi-Vari Study

Assume that samples of finished rope were taken in the following manner:

1. Three samples were taken per shift for three days (3 samples × 3 shifts × 3 days = 27 samples).
2. Specific sampling times were randomly taken, stratifying them to be 3 hours ± 1 hour apart.
3. A sample consisted of 30 continuous meters.
4. Each 30-meter sample was carefully cut into 10-meter segments and weighed, using the standard laboratory procedures for cutting and weighing. This provides 81 pieces of data (27 samples × 3 = 81).
5. Four test experiment situations were tabulated, in three-day segments of time. Figures I-1, I-2, I-3, and I-4 illustrate the four complete situation results for multi-vari analysis.

Refer to Figures I-1, I-2, I-3, and I-4. Each of the four figures represents four different situations. The evaluation should be on each individual figure. Study the plots, analyze them, and write down your conclusions about the meanings of the patterns of variation. After completing the analyses, turn to the solutions to see how close your conclusions are to

(Text continues on page 198.)

Figure I-1. First Multi-Vari Results.

(EACH TRIAD OF DOTS REPRESENTS 3 CONSECUTIVE LENGTHS.)

Figure I-2. Second Multi-Vari Results.

(EACH TRIAD OF DOTS REPRESENTS 3 CONSECUTIVE LENGTHS.)

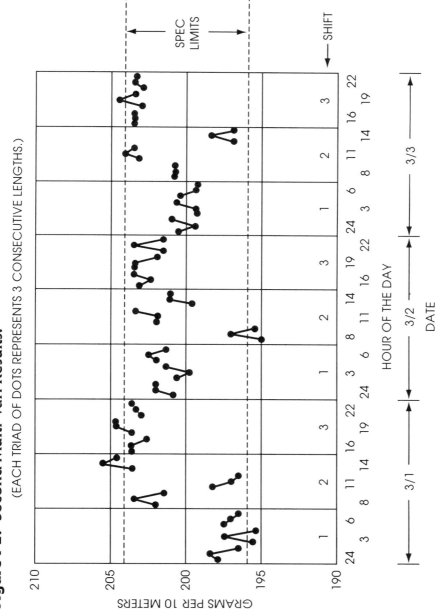

Figure I-3. Third Multi-Vari Results.
(EACH TRIAD OF DOTS REPRESENTS 3 CONSECUTIVE LENGTHS.)

Figure I-4. Fourth Multi-Vari Results.
(EACH TRIAD OF DOTS REPRESENTS 3 CONSECUTIVE LENGTHS.)

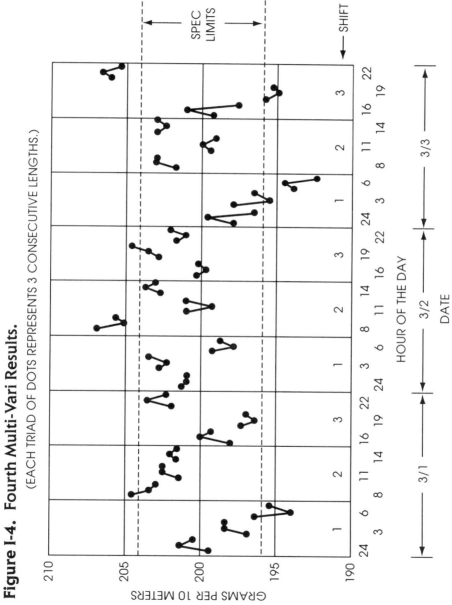

those given. For maximum learning benefit, do not look at the solutions until after you list yours.

Solutions

Figure I-1

There is little variation day to day or shift to shift, and there is no consistent pattern within a shift. The major pattern of variation is the large differences in the three 10-meter segments within each 30-meter sample. This pattern of variation rules out almost all the expected variables, primarily leaving measuring or weighing variation. This lack of repeatability between the three 10-meter segments could be due to erratic cutting of the 10-meter pieces—perhaps due to stretching as they are cut. Perhaps the weighing device has poor repeatability. The clues point to measuring, cutting, and weighing equipment and/or techniques.

A possible but less likely cause is rapid erratic changes (within 30 meters) such as lumps going through the process.

Figure I-2

The three 10-meter segments within the 30-meter samples are relatively consistent. The major pattern of variation is shift to shift. The second shift is erratic, while the first shift is consistent—although at different levels each day. The third shift is also consistent and is on the high side.

On the first two days when the first shift was not at the center of the specification, the second shift apparently overreacted by overcorrecting. One possibility is that the second shift is making large, frequent adjustments during its shift. Another possibility is that the first and third shifts are tightly controlling the process throughout the shift while the second shift is letting it wander all over.

The corrective actions are related to finding why one shift is consistent and within the shift although different each day, why one shift is consistent but high, and why second shift is erratic.

Figure I-3

Starting during the second shift of the first day and continuing through the next three shifts, the process was quite stable. Therefore, it would appear that the process is capable of doing far better than it is now doing.

There were four times that a large amount of variation and out-of-specification product occurred. In each case, the problem existed over approximately a 6-hour period. The fact that a tank of raw material lasts about 6 hours may suggest some possibilities to evaluate.

The second shift's average from day to day was more consistent than that of the two other shifts. On the second and third days early in the third shift, after the defects were very bad, the situation improved considerably. Did someone discover the problem and correct it? If so, capture this correction, make corrections earlier, and explain the correction to the other shifts.

Six out of seven times when the process shifted enough to go out of specification, the results jumped out abruptly. Was the cause of the extreme change in results something like the spinnerette clogging and unclogging?

Figure I-4

Generally there is a lot of variation within each shift. The process usually drifts downward. On five occasions, when the downward drift was corrected, a large correction (often too large) was made. If smaller corrections were made more frequently, the process would have far less variation.

Apparently second-shift employees crank up the process when they come in, whether or not the process needs it. The second shift tends to run on the high side. Have they learned that because of the downward drift they can start their run on the high side and make fewer adjustments?

On all three shifts two of the three sets of data are similar and the third set is different. This is an interesting observation, but its connection to the sources of variation is not so obvious. It is a weak clue but one that may bear further observation. Frequently, a weak clue such as this is negated by further data.

Conclusion

This study illustrates a complex process with many potentially important variables. Most designed experiments that might be considered would be very complex and difficult to run; therefore, it is important to run a multi-vari study to reduce the number of potential variables. Sometimes the clues from the multi-vari are strong and obvious enough to solve the problem or at least solve part of the problem. In other instances, the patterns of variation highlighted by the multi-vari study can eliminate most of the pet theories and their associated variables. Consequently, an experiment can be designed that includes only those few variables that fit the clues obtained from the multi-vari study.

Appendix II
Foundry Measles Charts

The Problem

A casting used in relatively high volume has experienced heavy losses due to porosity. Increasing customer demands will soon exceed production capacity unless a substantial reduction is made in the scrap rates. The customer is also pressing for a reduction in price, but the losses have kept costs quite high.

A task force composed of a foundry engineer, metallurgist, foundry superintendent, and quality engineer has been assigned to solve the problem. The quality engineer, who is the task force leader, is experienced in key variable isolation problem-solving strategies. With the task force, the quality engineer has established a 0 to 4 numerical rating scale to rank the degree of porosity. The engineer has prepared a form (see Figure II-1) on which results can be plotted in a measles chart style with separate results for cope and drag. Two identical castings are made in each mold and are shown next to each other on the form. The task force decides to perform a multi-vari study to evaluate the porosity problem.

The Multi-Vari Study

The multi-vari study consisted of taking three molds (six castings) in a row around 7 A.M. and another three molds near the end of the run, around 9 A.M. By plotting the porosity on the measles chart the size and location of the defects can be shown on a 1 to 4 scale. Because cope and drag (explained below) results are separated, within-piece (within-casting) variation

Figure II-1. Measles Chart Format.

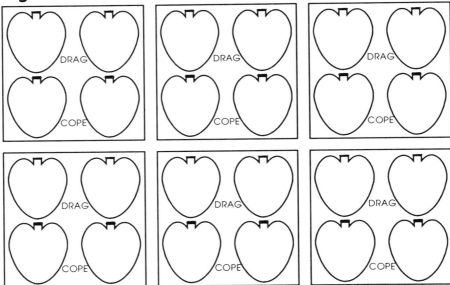

can be measured. Since there are two castings in a mold, within-mold variation can be examined. In addition, by taking three molds in a row, mold-to-mold variation can be shown, and by taking samples two times during the morning, time-to-time variation can be measured. The task force decides to run the study a second day to look at the day-to-day variation. In foundries, day-to-day differences are often a major problem.

There are four different sets of results. These are shown in Figures II-2, II-3, II-4, and II-5; each study reflects a different process condition, so each study should be evaluated separately. Figure II-2a shows results for the first day of study 1 and Figure II-2b shows results for day 2 of study 1. Figures II-3a and II-3b show the results for day 1 and day 2 of study 2, and so on.

In each square of the measles chart, the extreme upper left-hand heart-shaped picture illustrates the drag of one casting and another heart-shaped picture directly below illustrates the cope. The cope is the top half and the drag is the bottom half of the same casting; they are drawn separately so that the defects can be shown. The castings actually are lying down with the molten metal entering the gate in the *end* of the casting (the jagged part at the top of the picture is the gate; this gate is broken off after the casting has cooled). In the right side of the square is the cope and drag of the second casting that is poured in the same mold. The defects are shown as if the castings were transparent.

Each measles chart is labeled so as to indicate day, time, and mold number. For instance, in Figure II-2a the label 1-7-1 designates day 1, 7 A.M., mold number 1. The next square to the right contains four more heart-shaped pictures representing the two castings in the second mold. It is labeled Mold 1-7-2 (day 1, 7 A.M., mold 2). In the third square to the right, the third consecutive mold poured at 7 A.M. is labeled Mold 1-7-3 (day 1, 7 A.M., mold 3). The bottom half of Figure II-2a shows three more molds, poured at 9 A.M. (e.g., Mold 1-9-1 indicates day 1, 9 A.M., mold 1). The rest of the studies are numbered in the same manner.

At the top of each example is the defect score key for the measles charts. If the defect (porosity) is small (e.g., a "1"), there is a dot plotted on the measles chart. If the defect is larger (e.g., a "2") there is a circled dot. A "3" has a double circle and a "4" has a triple circle around the dot. In totaling defects (porosity) the numbers are simply added:

$$• \ + \ ◉ \ + \ • \ + \ ◎ \ = \ 7$$
$$1 \ + \ 2 \ + \ 1 \ + \ 3 \ = \ 7$$

Formulating the Study

For any of the four studies, day-to-day variation can be determined by totaling each of the two separate studies for day 1 and day 2. If all the 7 A.M. totals are compared to all the 9 A.M. totals, time-to-time variation can be determined. Also, mold-to-mold variation, casting-to-casting variation, and within-casting variation can be determined. It is possible to plot the results in a typical multi-vari chart, but a simple solution is to compare the total scores for all the patterns of variation. (A

(Text continues on page 208.)

Figure II-2. Casting Porosity Study 1.

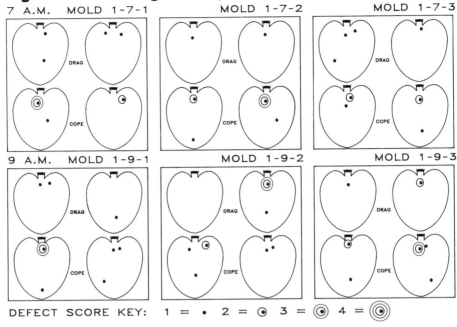

Figure II-2a. Study 1, Day 1.

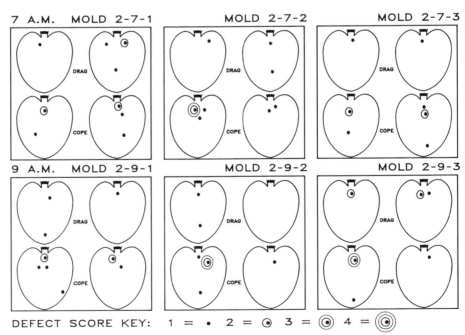

Figure II-2b. Study 1, Day 2.

Figure II-3. Casting Porosity Study 2.

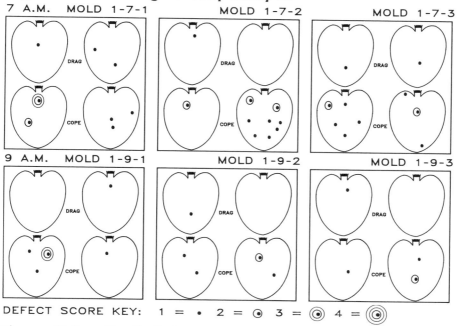

Figure II-3a. Study 2, Day 1.

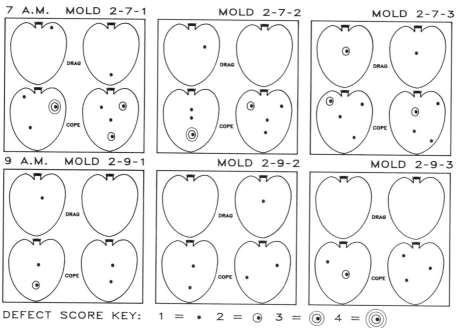

Figure II-3b. Study 2, Day 2.

Figure II-4. Casting Porosity Study 3.

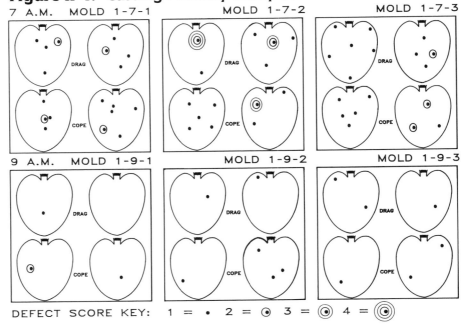

DEFECT SCORE KEY: 1 = •   2 = ⊙   3 = ◉   4 = ◎

Figure II-4a. Study 3, Day 1.

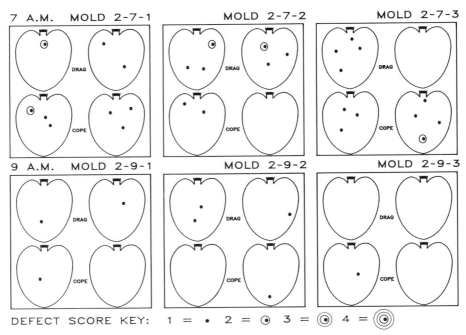

DEFECT SCORE KEY: 1 = •   2 = ⊙   3 = ◉   4 = ◎

Figure II-4b. Study 3, Day 2.

Figure II-5. Casting Porosity Study 4.

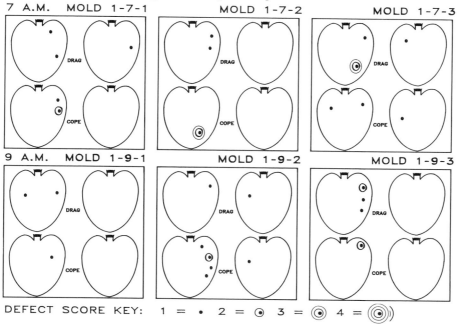

Figure II-5a. Study 4, Day 1.

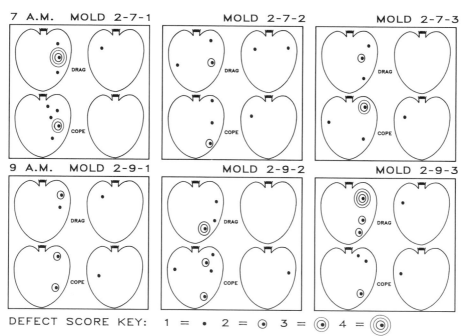

Figure II-5b. Study 4, Day 2.

multi-vari chart for study 3 is shown a little later on in Figure II-7.)

If, for example, the total score for all 7 A.M. readings of one study was 80 and for 9 A.M. the total was 40, you could then conclude that there was twice as high a defect (porosity) score at 7 A.M. as there was at 9 A.M. The next step would be to consider what could cause more porosity first thing in the morning—at the beginning of the run—as compared to two hours later at the end of the run. Causes of the problem might include metal temperature, sand temperature, humidity, operator alertness, and so on. Each study includes more than one clue.

The "task force" (i.e., *you*) should review the results and decide which pattern(s) of variation stand out and by how much. Once these determinations are made, the task force should try to determine which variables best fit the clues.

Assignment

Your assignment is to review the four studies illustrated by Figures II-2 through II-5 to determine which patterns of variation stand out and by how much. Then, consider what might be done next.

Solutions

Study 1

The total defect score for the upper half of the castings in the measles charts (both cope and drag) is 96 and the lower half is 24, a ratio of four to one.

On the other hand, if the measles chart is cut into four sections as shown in Figure II-6 an even larger difference (96 to 1) can be seen between the portion nearest the gate (the upper section of the picture where the metal flows in) and the left section.

The causes of high defect score for the upper quarter of the castings (near the gate) might include the turbulence of the

Figure II-6. Division of Casting.

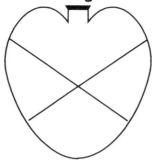

metal entering the gate trapping gases (possibly due to pour-ing too fast or to too much constriction in the gate area). Also, slag might be floating on the metal near the gate.

In another comparison, the total defect score in study 1 in the cope was twice as high as in the drag (80 to 40), a ratio of 2 to 1. With a 2-to-1 ratio of cope versus drag, perhaps trapped gases could not escape and were caught in the top half of the casting (cope); maybe better venting is needed. Or perhaps slag floating on the top of the metal caused more porosity in the cope.

Study 2

In study 2 the 7 A.M. defect score total was 73 and the 9 A.M. total was 35, just over a 2-to-1 ratio. The cope totaled 91 and the drag totaled 17, a ratio of almost 5.4 to 1.

The 7 A.M. scores might be twice as high as the 9 A.M. scores because of metal temperature, sand temperature, hu-midity, operator alertness, ambient temperature, daily startup problems, and so forth. Problems such as these might be over-come by 9 A.M. The 5.4-to-1 defect score ratio of cope to drag might be due to causes similar to those in study 1, that is, trapped gases, floating slag, or the necessity for better venting.

Study 3

In study 3 the total defect score for 7 A.M. was 97 and at 9 A.M. it was 24, a ratio of about 4 to 1. The first-day defect score

totaled 80 and the second day totaled 41, a ratio of about 2 to
1. The 7 A.M. defect score might be four times as high as 9 A.M.
for the same reasons as in study 2: problems encountered at 7
A.M. had been overcome by 9 A.M.

In contrast, the 2-to-1 defect score ratio of day 1 versus
day 2 suggests other possibilities. Possibly day 1 was a Monday
startup after a weekend shutdown with its associated weekly
startup problems; possibly different crews, metallurgical differences, metal temperature, sand temperature and humidity,
ambient temperature and humidity, crew alertness the first
day of the week, and so forth affected the results.

Study 4

In study 4, day 1 had a defect score of 35 and day 2 had a defect
score of 71 for a ratio of about 1 to 2. Also, the left castings
(including cope and drag) had a score of 91 while the right
castings (cope and drag) had a score of 15, a ratio of over
6 to 1.

If the left side of all castings is compared to the right side
of all castings, there is a difference of about 5.2 to 1; the right
side total is 89 and the left side total is 17. This result is influenced by the 6-to-1 ratio between the left and right castings in
the mold (91 to 15). However, if the observer adds the left side
of the left castings to the right side of the right castings, he will
obtain a total of 8 for the "outside half" of the two castings. If
he adds the right side of the left castings to the left side of the
right castings, he will get a total of 98 for the "inside half" of
the two castings. Thus, there is a ratio of over 12 to 1 comparing the "inside" versus the "outside." This large ratio could
easily be missed, partly because the 6-to-1 defect score ratio of
the left casting versus the right casting tends to overshadow or
mask this big difference. The comparison of "inside" versus
"outside" is practical because the "inside" is more likely to
retain heat, as a result of the castings being next to each other.
The "outside" half could cool much more quickly, and the resulting temperature differential could cause defects.

Causes of the 6-to-1 defect score ratio from the left casting
to the right casting could be attributed to pattern design and

construction, because these two castings are supposed to be identical; they have the same sand, same metal, same crew, and so forth. Causes of the 1-to-2 ratio of day 1 to day 2 might be somewhat similar to the possible causes in study 3 of the 2-to-1 ratio from day 1 to day 2 except that because day 2 is higher, the possible causes are not related to startup, but rather to the differences between one day and the next.

Further Study

It is appropriate to analyze these four multi-vari studies completely only by adding the totals as we have already done. The investigator could, however, plot the results. For instance, in Figure II-7 the total defect scores (cope and drag combined) for the castings in study 3 are shown on a multi-vari chart. The day 1, 7 A.M., mold 1 castings have defect scores of 10 (left casting) and 12 (right casting). These two defect scores are

Figure II-7. Multi-Vari for Study 3 Data.

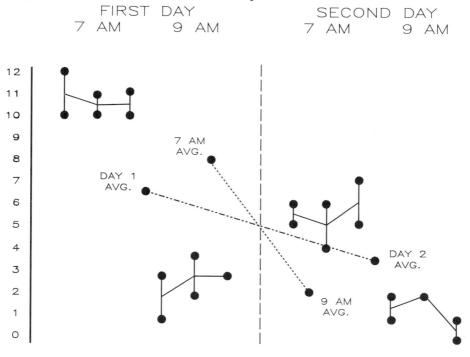

plotted and are connected by a vertical line. In mold 2 the left casting totals 10 and the right casting totals 11; these two defect scores are plotted and connected to represent the score in the second mold. Similarly, the defect scores in mold 3 of 11 and 10 are plotted and connected. The mold 1, mold 2, and mold 3 averages are connected to represent the results at 7 A.M. on day 1.

A similar plot is made for the 9 A.M. results for day 1 and then the 7 A.M. and 9 A.M. results are plotted for day 2. All of these four sets of plots are captioned at the top of the figure. Then all the 7 A.M. results (day 1, 7 A.M., and day 2, 7 A.M.) are averaged, plotted with a dot halfway between the two sets of 7 A.M. plots, and labeled 7 A.M. *Avg.* Also, the 9 A.M. results (for both days) are averaged, plotted with a dot halfway between the two sets of plots, and labeled 9 A.M. *Avg.* A dotted line between these two dots shows the 7 A.M. to 9 A.M. difference.

Similarly, the day 1 results are averaged, plotted with a dot halfway between the two sets of day 1 plots, and labeled *Day 1 Avg.* The same procedure is done with the day 2 plots and labeled *Day 2 Avg.* These two dots are connected with a dashed line to highlight the difference between the two days. The dotted line connecting the 7 A.M. average to the 9 A.M. average has a greater difference than the dashed line connecting *Day 1 Avg.* to *Day 2 Avg.* because the 7 A.M. to 9 A.M. defect score ratio was 4 to 1, while the day 1 to day 2 defect score ratio was 2 to 1.

These studies are not necessarily meant to be practical for detecting what causes porosity. The purpose is to give the reader an opportunity to practice the multi-vari approach and to determine patterns of variation that provide clues as to which variables may cause problems. These variables become prime candidates for other studies including a designed experiment, often the next step in the key variable isolation problem-solving strategy.

Glossary

The definitions of words and terms in this glossary are not intended to set standards for usage but to clarify the meaning of the word or term as it is used in this book.

analysis of variance (ANOVA) A statistical procedure used for analyzing designed experiments. ANOVA compares mean square variation due to variables and interactions (the signal) to mean square variation due to residual error (noise). The purpose of ANOVA is to see if the variation in the experiment attributable to the variables and/or interactions is large enough to stand out above the variation in the residual, that is, variation not explainable by the variables and interactions under investigation. The statistical mathematical procedure for performing ANOVA is complex but software is available to do the calculations. The theory and procedure of ANOVA are presented in numerous texts on statistical analysis and designed experiments, such as Wilfred J. Dixon and Frank J. Massey, Jr., *Introduction to Statistical Analysis* (New York: McGraw-Hill Book Company, Inc., 1983).

attributes Product characteristics that are visual, pertaining to workmanship, or cosmetic rather than dimensional in nature. Attributes are usually designated as "good" or "bad," "acceptable" or "unacceptable," "satisfactory" or "unsatisfactory." In the key variable isolation strategy, attributes are always quantified by applying a numerical scale to them.

capping run A production run made after various testing is completed to verify that the conclusions drawn are correct.

clock diagram A graphic representation of an object or condition plotted as though it were on the face of a clock. The roundness and surface condition of circular or cylindrical objects, such as crankshaft journals, and patterns, such as the wavefront propagation from an antenna, are often plotted on clock diagrams or similar graphs. Measurements are made at numerous locations and are plotted on the diagram. A zero reference line (or point) is plotted on the diagram, and deviations—plus or minus—of out-of-plane, out-of-round, or eccentricity are plotted around the "clock" face. If out-of-round were being plotted and there was no measurable out-of-round, the plot would show all points on the zero reference line. The clock diagram provides a graphic picture of the amount and direction of the deviation from a perfect product or condition.

component search   A testing technique that uses an assembly that is functioning very well and an assembly that is functioning very badly. These assemblies are first tested separately and the results recorded. Then, the component search process is started by exchanging parts (components) between the two assemblies. The first component exchanged is the one that is believed to be the most likely cause of the difference in performance. The two assemblies with the exchanged components are then tested again. This exchange of components can produce a variety of results, such as:

1. The results of the testing after the component was exchanged are about the same as they were before the component was exchanged, suggesting that the suspected component is not the cause of the problem (i.e., not the key variable).

2. The results are about the same as those from the previous testing except the results are reversed. That is, when the most suspect component was changed, the results changed with it, which means that the first component chosen for exchange is the cause of the difference in performance.

3. The results are somewhere between the above two results, that is, the better assembly became somewhat degraded and the poorer assembly became somewhat better. These results indicate that the first component chosen is important but that there are other important ones as well. The degree by which the results fall between the two results above indicates the relative importance of the most suspect component. If one set of results changes but not the other, or both get better or both get worse, this indicates an interaction in which the effect of one component depends on which assembly it is in.

In component search, the first few exchanges are made one component at a time. However, after these exchanges are made, several components may be exchanged at the same time to speed up the process. The process of exchanging components continues until all the important exchanges have been made, that is, the original test result differences between the two assemblies have been switched from one assembly to the other. Then the industrial investigator returns to the original configuration of components and repeats the test to see if the original test results are obtained. The purpose of returning to the original configuration is to ensure that other unknown factors have not changed during the time the tests were run.

The analysis of a component search procedure is generally done by plotting the data rather than by elaborate calculations.

fast-shot length   In aluminum die-casting, the injection cycle consists of a slow phase, an acceleration phase, and a fast phase. The fast-shot length is the distance the plunger travels during the fast phase as it injects molten aluminum into the die cavity.

fast-shot velocity   In aluminum die-casting, the injection cycle consists of a slow phase, an acceleration phase, and a fast phase. The fast-shot velocity is the speed at which the plunger travels during the phase as it injects molten aluminum into the die cavity.

flash   An overfilled condition that results in thin excess plastic attached to a molded plastic product at die lines, parting lines, and knock-out pin bosses.

fractional factorial designed experiment   An experiment in which only a carefully selected number of all the levels of variables are tested. Fewer tests are required than with full factorial experiments, resulting in the loss of some information about potential interactions.

framing or bracketing   The process of identifying the types or classes of variables that are causing the greatest variation.

full factorial designed experiment   An experiment in which every combination of all levels of all variables is tested.

industrial investigator   A person or team that applies the tools, techniques, and strategies of key variable isolation to learn which variables or interactions are at the root of a product problem.

isoplot   A graph on which the X (horizontal) scale represents the readings of one inspector or instrument and the Y (vertical) scale represents the readings of a second inspector or instrument. An isoplot is used to graphically represent the agreement of these two sets of readings. For example, if the second inspector obtained exactly the same reading as the first inspector on all units being measured, the points would all be plotted on the 45-degree line of perfect agreement. Points not on the 45-degree line indicate disagreement between readings.

measles chart   A pictorial representation of a product where the location and degree of defects are plotted. For instance, if all the defects on a product were on the left side, the measles chart would have all the spots plotted on the left side, often shown in red. These red spots would give the product the appearance of having measles on the left side. This concentration of defects in one area would suggest causes that are capable of affecting only part of the product and would rule out variables that could not produce defects on one side only. Measles charts are often used with a multi-vary study to further define within-piece variation. Measles charts are also called concentration diagrams.

median chart   A median chart is an alternative to the average or X-bar chart. On a median chart the middle, or median, number or value is plotted, thus eliminating the need to calculate the average. For example, if 4, 5, and 8 are measurements made on three parts, the average, or 5.7, would be plotted on an X-bar chart, and the median number, or 5, would be plotted on a median chart. The median chart control limits are calculated differently from X-bar chart control limits. A median chart is less subject to being greatly influenced by one number that is considerably higher or lower than the other numbers in the sample. See Eugene L. Grant and Richard S. Leavenworth, *Statistical Quality Control* (New York: McGraw-Hill Book Company, Inc., 1987).

multiple balance   A form of fractional factorial experiment in which a small number of all variables at all levels are tested. Multiple balance is similar to random balance; however, within the overall test design, one or more full factorial experiments are run together while the levels of all the other variables are chosen randomly. The analysis of a multiple balance test is done in total as in a random balance test, but the full factorial formats within the experiment are analyzed separately as any other full factorial experiment would be. Multiple balance is often considered a screening test because there is the potential for missing some interactions. (See also **random balance**.)

multi-vari study   A stratified sampling study that looks at multiple types of variables. The data are collected to yield a pattern of variation including within-piece, piece-to-piece, time-to-time, and often other patterns such as machine-to-machine and batch-to-batch. Once the key pattern is recognized, most variables that are guessed at can be eliminated because those variables could not produce the pattern of defects observed. For example, it may be speculated that the raw material is a key variable, but the defects occur only on the upper left part of a symmetrical product. Raw material variation does not fit that clue. A multi-vary study does not interfere with or interrupt production, and it often solves the problem of excessive product variation. In other cases, the multi-vary study rules out most of the guessed-at variables and leaves a small number of variables that fit the clues on the multi-vari plot. These few variables are then studied in detail, usually with a designed experiment.

numerical scale   The numbers assigned to varying levels of quality for a product characteristic that is visual, pertaining to workmanship, or cosmetic. Developing a numerical scale is a prerequisite for running a multi-vari study. A numerical scale can also be a tool for judging the effect of process changes, for monitoring quality trends of a process, and for auditing the output of a process.

open-ended questions   In this book, open-ended questions are contrasted to closed-ended questions. A closed-ended question might be, "Is temperature the key variable?" An open-ended question might be, "Does the pattern of variation indicate that the key variable causes variation within the piece, piece to piece, time to time, or machine to machine, and so forth?" The answer to an open-ended question is usually a type or class of variables that tends to rule out those variables that have a pattern of variation that does not agree with the observed pattern of variation.

percent defective   The portion of manufactured products that is determined not to meet specifications. If, for example, 200 products are made and 30 of these are defective, the production run would be 15% defective.

piece-to-piece variation   Variation from one piece to the next piece. Piece-to-piece variation analysis is typically performed on consecutive pieces as they come from a machine or production line. Piece-to-piece variation often suggests random variation in the operation, variation introduced from earlier processes, and/or measurement error. The evidence of excessive piece-to-piece variation usually rules out process variables such as temperature and raw material because these variables are unlikely to change between the production of consecutive pieces.

process latitude study   A study done to determine the tolerances (or latitude) appropriate for process input variables. The study is run by setting process input variables at the limits of the current specification and testing to see what effect these settings have on the process output. For example, if the process latitude study shows that operating with a process input variable, such as temperature, set at its high limit creates too much variation in a product dimension, such as length, then the operating tolerance limits for temperature must be reduced. Conversely, if varying the process input variable from the maximum to the minimum tolerance has no measurable effect on the output, then the tolerance can be opened up and retested to set new, wider tolerance limits.

pull test   A tensile test in which a specified force is applied to a feature such as a welded or soldered joint or to the lead of an electronic component. The joint or component is then tested to see if it still meets the requirements.

random balance   A form of fractional factorial experiment in which only a small fraction of the total number of combinations of all variables at all levels is tested. The selection of which combination of variables is tested at which levels is done randomly. Balance is achieved by performing the same number of tests at each variable condition. As with any fractionalized experiment, the opportunity to evaluate some interactions is lost. However, less rigidity in planning and execution is required compared to classical fractional factorials. Random balance is most effective as a screening test that looks for the major factors influencing variation.

random number table   A set of randomly selected numbers in which each number has an equal and independent chance to be selected. Random numbers are used to design tests or experiments so as to reduce or eliminate the effects of shifts, trends, cyclical variation, or other forms of bias during sampling or test evaluation. See Wilfrid J. Dixon and Frank J. Massey, Jr., *Introduction to Statistical Analysis* (New York: McGraw-Hill Book Company, Inc., 1983).

repeat   A process operation that is performed more than once without changing process input settings or conditions.

replication   A test condition in which process input variables are set to levels different from a previous run, the process is run with the new settings, and then the settings are reset to the original settings and the process is rerun. A replicate is different from a repeat. A replicate only occurs if other combinations of variables are run and then the process is reset to the original combination of variables to run the subsequent replicate. (Compare with **repeat**.)

short shot   A condition caused by injecting an insufficient amount of plastic into a mold cavity, resulting in an incompletely molded part. (The term *short shot* is also used in die casting and molten metal injection.)

splay   An elongated, silvery surface imperfection on a molded plastic product that sometimes appears as an unusually high-gloss area or minor delamination. Splay is usually caused by volatiles (moisture, monomer, degradation products, etc.) in the melt stream in the form of bubbles that fracture at the surface of the cavity during the injection phase of the cycle.

stratified sampling   The selection of samples from a process based on a plan that provides the most likelihood of showing variation from piece to piece, time to time, shift to shift, machine to machine, and so on. (Within-piece variation can be determined from either stratified or random sampling.) A stratified sample provides the most information on patterns of variation with the smallest number of samples. A random sample, on the other hand, is intended to give an unbiased indication of quality on an already produced lot of products often for the purpose of deciding to accept or reject the lot of material.

time-to-time variation   Variation in a product from one time period to another time period, either short term or longer term.

type or class of variables   That portion of the entire list of process input variables that causes common patterns of variation. For example, if the greatest variation is from first shift to second shift, then the type or class of variables for further investigation would include only those variables that can vary from first shift to second shift.

variables   Process parameters such as temperature, pressure, time, speed, and so forth. This usage should not be confused with variables inspection, which refers to using measured product characteristics. It is generally accepted that process variables can vary within limits without causing excessive variation in the product made by the process. When a process variable varies excessively, or if it is set to an inappropriate level (e.g., temperature set too high), that condition causes the product to be defective. The process variable is then referred to as a *key* variable.

variables search   A technique by which the levels or settings of process variables are exchanged between "good" and "bad" levels. Variables search is similar to component search except that settings of process variables, rather than components, are exchanged.

variation   The difference in quality, performance, or measurement between two or more products or conditions. The difference in the weights of two packages of frozen food, for example, would be called the variation in weight. Variation can occur in one of two categories: acceptable variation (i.e., variation within or less than specified limits) or excessive variation. Excessive variation is considered symptomatic of process problems caused by one or more key process variables.

void An internal imperfection in a molded plastic product, which resembles a bubble but contains a near vacuum instead of being pressurized. A void is usually the result of phase shrinkage (transition from a fluid phase to a solid phase) and thermal shrinkage during the cooling phase of the cycle. Typically, a void is found in thick-walled areas which, during cooling, form rigid skins capable of supporting the negative internal pressure that develops as the liquid center continues to cool.

within-piece variation Variation that exists in the dimension or physical appearance of the same feature of the same part or piece, that is, from end to end, side to side, top to bottom, and so on. Excessive within-piece variation, such as out of round, taper, location of air entrapment, foreign material location, and deformed shape, often is caused by peculiarities of the manufacturing equipment or process such as misalignment, inadequate venting, or poor die design. Evidence of within-piece variation rules out many process variables that could not change within one piece.

Bibliography

Book

Bhote, Keki R., *World Class Quality*. New York: AMACOM, 1991.

Periodicals

Gunter, Berton H., "Graphical Data Analysis," Statistics Corner, *Quality Progress*, May 1988, pp. 62–63.

Pollard, John, "Unusual Ways to Reduce Costs," *Steel Founders Society of America, Steel Foundry Facts,* January 1972.

Seder, L. A., "Diagnosis With Diagrams," *Industrial Quality Control,* January 1950.

Shainin, Dorian, "The Statistically Designed Experiment," *Harvard Business Review,* July–August 1957, pp. 67–73.

Traver, Robert W., "Quality Control—How Much Is Enough?" *Management Review,* April 1970, pp. 36–39.

Traver, Robert W., "Locating the Key Variable(s)," *Quality Progress,* February 1984, pp. 21–27.

Traver, Robert W., "A Funny Thing Happened on the Way to Inspection," *Tooling & Production Magazine,* June 1971.

Traver, Robert W., "Pre-Control—A Good Alternative to $\overline{X}$-R Charts," *Quality Progress,* September 1985, pp. 11–14.

Unpublished Reports

Desrosiers, Victor J., "Final Report of Process Controls on Performance," unpublished report to New York State Science and Technology Foundation regarding Contract No. PDP (87)-5, November 20, 1987.

Traver, Robert W., "Final Report on Hot Crank Investigation," unpublished report to Pontiac Motor Division, General Motors Corporation, March 1, 1967.

Unpublished Book

Rath & Strong, Inc., *Quality Assurance Handbook*. Lexington, Mass.: 1970–1971.

Transactions

Barker, Thomas B., "Quality Engineering by Design—The Taguchi Approach," in *Quality Congress Transactions*. Baltimore: American Society for Quality Control, 1985.

Traver, Robert W. "Measuring Equipment Repeatability—The Rubber Ruler," in *Annual Convention Transactions*. Cincinnati: American Society for Quality Control, 1962.

Index

acceptability levels, numerical rating scale and, 14
accountability of corporate departments, 142
accuracy, defining with isoplot, 95
aluminum die-casting case study, 123–139
  cleaning project, 127–130, 136–137
  machining for, 130–131
  measles chart of defects, 125
  multi-vari study on contaminants, 128–129
  quality improvement project for, 124–127
analysis of variance (ANOVA), 85–86, 179, 213
anechoic room, 105–106
artillery projectiles case study, 46–54
  designed experiment for, 48–51
attitudes, engineers' openness to change, 67–70
attributes, 13, 213
  quantification of, 14–15

balance in designed experiments, 32–33
biased data
  isoplot of, 95–96
  observed, 92–93

bimodal distribution, 144
  as indicator of within-batch variation, 145
bore defects, 74–81
  designed experiment for, 74–80
  multi-vari study of, 74–76
bracketing, 215
brainstorming, 4, 151, 176

capital improvements, 188
capping run, 213
case studies
  aluminum die-casting, 123–139
  artillery projectiles, 46–54
  coil resistance, 18–21
  disc punch, 150–154
  dust cover seals, 55–60
  electronic component pull strength, 180–181
  flat beer, 25–31
  foundry casting porosity, 201–212
  hot crank car, 160–173
  injection-mold scrap rate, 175–180
  noisy motors, 102–111
  nondisintegrating tablets, 140–149
  porous rings, 38–45
  semiconductor chips, 184–186

case studies (*continued*)
  solid-state devices, 112–122
  spline demerits, 155–159
  stopper leaks, 82–90
casting, *see* aluminum die-cast
  case study
cavity-to-cavity variation, 62
class of variables, 218
cleaning of aluminum die-cast
  part, 127–130, 136–137
clock diagrams, 133, 153, 213
clouded plotted points, 93, 97
clues
  in dust cover seals case study,
    57–59
  from motor noise study, 107–
    110
  in multi-vari technique, 11
coil resistance case study, 18–21
component printing defect
  scores, noise and, 35–37
components, switching during
  testing, 165
component search, 214–215
confidence level, 37
  significance level for, 86
consensus for rating scale, 16
consultants, 1–2
consulting with the process, 30
contaminants, in aluminum die-
  cast part, 127
correlation, perfect, 92

data evaluation in multi-vari
  studies, 19–20
  exercises, 189–212
day-to-day variation, 203
deductive skills, 1
defective products, 2–3
  locating source with parallel
    path process, 184–186

overstress testing for low
  rates, 83
designed experiments, 32–37
  for aluminum casting, 124–
    127
  for artillery projectiles, 48–51
  for bore defects, 76–80
  elements of, 32
  extremes in, 48
  full factorial, 176, 179, 215
  for hot crank car case study,
    165–167
  noise in, 34
  in nondisintegrating tablets
    case study, 146–148
  for porous rings, 42–44
  for seat dimension of forged
    part, 70–71
  statistical analysis of, 37
  for stopper leaks case study,
    84–85
  vs. multi-vari studies, 11–12
  wrong variables in, 34
  see also fractional factorial de-
    signed experiments
dial indicator gauge, 131
dimensional analysis, 107
dimensional variation, reducing, 62
diminishing returns, 116, 169
disc punch case study, 150–154
  engineering approach to, 151
  multi-vari studies for, 152
dust cover seals case study, 55–
  60
  using clues, 57–59
  dynamometer testing, 168–
    171

eccentricity, 150
electric motor noise case study,
  102–111

clue evaluation from, 107–110
multi-vari study for, 103–107
electronic component pull
    strength case study, 180–
    181
engineering
    statistical, xiii
    as traditional approach to
        problem solving, 4–5, 66–
        72
    traditional vs. key variable
        isolation, 59
engineers, openness to change,
    67–70
engine-to-engine variation, 171
equipment, need for new, 188
experiments
    coordinating with manage-
        ment, 28
    running, 28–29
    see also designed experiments
experts
    comparing quality control in-
        spector ratings with, 94–96
    panel to create rating scale,
        16–17
extremes, in designed experi-
    ments, 48

faced surfaces, maintaining
    plane, 132–134, 138–139
fast-shot length, 215
fast-shot velocity, 215
flash, 215
flat beer case study, 25–31
forged part seat dimension, 66–
    73
foundry, measles charts for,
    201–212
fractional factorial designed ex-
    periments, 215

for multicavity compression
    molder, 63
vs. random balance, 116–117
framing, 215
full factorial designed experi-
    ments, 176, 179, 215
functional gauge, 155, 157

graphical analysis, xiii
    clock diagrams, 133, 153, 213
    scatter plots, 118, 120
    see also isoplots; measles chart

hot crank car case study, 160–
    173
    analysis of testing, 169–171
    designed experiment for,165–
        167
    initiation of study, 161–162
    terminology, 161
    testing procedure, 162–165

imprecise data isoplot, 93, 96
improvements, evaluating, 113
inaccurate observed data, 92–93
inductive skills, 1
industrial investigator, 215
industrial problem solving, ix
information, on product prob-
    lems, 3
injection-mold scrap rate
    case study, 175–180
    splay problems, 175, 179–180,
        218
    void problems, 175, 176–179,
        219
inspection of products, 7
    rate for, 43–44
    saving in time, 129
interactions, 48, 49, 52–53
    in designed experiments, 33
    determining significance, 86

interactions (*continued*)
  indicator of, 78–80
  of key variables, 22–24, 29
  of multiple factors, 147–148
  plot intersection for, 87–88
internal customers, variation
    impacting, 66
internship method to learn key
    variable isolation, 5–6
intersect of plots, 87–88
isoplots, 91–101, 215
  measuring bias on, 95–96
  of noise measurement, 104–
    105
  using, 94–96

job shops, 132

key variable isolation, xiv, 1–6
  advantages of, 5
  defining, 3
  learning, 5–6
  parallel path experimentation
    for, 183
  training, 123
  using multi-vari, x
  vs. traditional engineering ap-
    proach, 59, 66–72
key variables, 3
  determining cause of problem
    from multiple, 32
  interactions of, 22–24, 29
  screening test for, 114
knit line, in stoppers, 83

lubricants, 147

machine-to-machine variation,
    48
machining, for aluminum die-
    cast, 130–131, 137–138

maldistribution principle, in Pa-
    reto concept, 114, 116
management, 74
  coordinating experiments
    with, 28
manufacturing department, vs.
    quality control department,
    142
manufacturing problem, turning
    on and off, 52
manufacturing processes, varia-
    tion, 2–3
markets, 20
market share, specification and,
    150
measles chart, 39, 40, 41, 215–
    216
  for casting defects, 125
  for foundry, 201–212
measurements
  data for isoplot, 91
  for hot crank problem, 161
  need for objective system, 105
  repeatability and reproducibil-
    ity, 105, 131
measurement tools
  dial indicator gauge, 131
  dynamometer, 168–171
  functional gauge, 155, 157
  pointed micrometer, 67
  uncalibrated, 93
  vernier caliper, 67
median chart, 216
micrometer, pointed, 67
molded plastic components,
    multicavity-forming ma-
    chines for, 61–65
mold-to-mold variation, 203
multicavity-forming machines,
    for molded plastic compo-
    nents, 61–65
multiple balance test design,
    121–122, 216

multi-vari study(ies), xiv, 3, 7–12, 216–217
  for artillery projectiles, 46–48
  of bore defects, 74–76
  on casting contaminants, 128–129
  clues in, 11
  on coil resistance, 18–21
  data evaluation, 19–20
  vs. designed experiments, 11–12
  for disc eccentricity, 152
  for electric motor noise, 103–107
  to evaluate variables controlling process, 175–176
  exercises, 189–212
  of foundry casting, 201–212
  of machining, 130–131
  for multicavity compression molder, 61–64
  in nondisintegrating tablets case study, 144–146
  of out-of-plane condition, 133–134
  polyester rope process, 193–200
  for porous rings, 39
  for seat measurements, 67–70
  for spline demerits, 156
  for stopper leaks case study, 83
  vs. variables search, 174
myths, 43

noise
  in experiment, 3
  see also electric motor noise case study
nondisintegrating tablets
  case study, 140–149
  designed experiment in, 146–148

  multi-vari study in, 144–146
  quantification in, 143–144
nonparallel response, 80
  in interaction plot, 87
normal curve, 144
numerical rating scale, 14, 187, 217
  for aluminum porosity, 124
  for cleanliness, 128
  for ring porosity, 39
  for visual defects, 61

observed data, for isoplot, 91
open-ended questions, 217
operator
  control of quality, 131
  responsibility level for problems, 67, 113, 187
optimization, 139
overstress testing, for low defect rates, 83

parallel path experimentation, 183–186
Pareto chart, 55, 56
  for hot crank cars, 168
Pareto concept, 82, 114–117
  combining with sampling theory, 116
pass testing, 143
percent defective calculations, 14, 217
perfect correlation, 92
personnel, meeting with problem-solving team, 74
piece-to-piece variation, 9, 10, 47, 48, 217
  in aluminum die-cast contaminants, 128
  in disc punch, 152
  in spline demerits, 156

place-to-place variation, in tab-
    let disintegration, 145
plane, maintaining for faced
    surfaces, 132–134, 138–139
planning, 26–28
plants, evaluating standards of,
    112–122
plastic molding operation, 55–
    60
point of diminishing returns,
    116
pointed micrometer, 67
polyester rope manufacturing
    process, exercise, 191–200
porous rings case study, 38–45
    designed experiment for, 42–
        44
    quantification in, 38–39
precontrol strategy, 131–132
pressure, interaction with tem-
    perature, 22–24
problems
    correction after experiment,
        29–30
    operator level of responsibility
        for, 67, 113, 187
problem solving, ix
    advantages of strategies, 134–
        135
    group involvement in, 26
    planning approach, 25–26
    success in, 53
    traditional engineering ap-
        proach, 4–5
    traditional vs. key variable
        isolation, 59, 66–72
problem-solving team, meeting
    with, 74
problem-solving testing, vs.
    product-acceptance-pass
    testing, 155

process
    consulting with, 30
    determining separate, 61
    evaluating variables control-
        ling, 175–176
process control, 129–130, 131–
    132
process input variable, 3
process latitude study, 63, 217
process variables, *see* variables
product-acceptance-pass test-
    ing, vs. problem-solving
    testing, 155
product characteristics, quantifi-
    cation of, 13
production lines, finding prob-
    lem point in, 183–186
production schedules, 134
products
    inspection of, 7
    variation in, 2–3, *see also* varia-
        tion
psychological benefits, 26
pull test, 180, 218

quality audit, 30
quality control department, vs.
    manufacturing department,
    142
quality control inspector, com-
    paring ratings with expert,
    94–96
quality improvement program,
    123–134
quantification, 13–17
    of attributes, 14–15
    of disc eccentricity, 151–152
    methods for leaks, 82–83
    in porous ring case study, 38–
        39
    in problem-solving approach,
        26

in tablet disintegration case study, 143–144

random balance, 113, 116–117, 218
  analysis of example test data, 118–120
  example of, 117–121
  number of variables, 117
  purpose of, 114
randomization, 85
  in designed experiment, 49, 76–77
  in variables search test, 174
random number table, 51, 118, 218
random variation, 115
ratings, comparing those of quality control inspector and expert, 94–96
raw material, 187
  multi-vari study and, 144
  problems in tablets from, 142–143
  quality, 121
reading-to-reading variation, 131
recalibration, 16
reference data, for isoplot, 91
refining, 16
repeatability, 218
  in gauge evaluation, 155
  in hot crank car problem, 161–162, 170
  lack of, 198
  of measurements, 105
  in random balance, 118
  vs. replication, 77
replication, 218
  number to test, 51
  runs for, 118
  vs. repeats, 77

reproducibility
  in gauge evaluation, 155
  of measurements, 105
residual error, 33–35
responsibility for problem, operator and, 67, 113, 187
review of operations, 113
rework rates, 134
root cause of problem, defining, ix–x

sample size, 114
sampling, stratified, 113, 218
sampling procedure, 62
sampling theory, 113–114
  combining with Pareto concept, 116
Satterthwaite, Frank, 113, 116
scale of diminishing returns, 169
scatter plots, for random balance experiment, 118, 120
scrap rates, 38, 134
  of foundry, 201
  from injection-mold process, 175–180
screening test, 114
seam in stopper, 83
seat dimension of forged part, 66–73
  designed experiment for, 70–71
  multi-vari study for, 67–70
Seder, Leonard, 7
semiconductor chips case, 184–186
setup plan, precontrol for, 132
shift-to-shift variation, 48, 128, 130–131
short shot, 218
solid-state devices case study, 112–122
  random balance technique for, 120–121

specifications, 20, 121
  for cleanliness, 127
  levels for quality control, 142
  limits for variables, 63
  relaxation of, 110, 127
  tolerances and precontrol, 132
splay in injection-mold product,
      175, 218–219
  correcting, 179–180
spline demerits case study, 155–
      159
  multi-vari study in, 156
standards, evaluating for manu-
      facturing plants, 112–122
startup rejects, in injection-mold
      process, 175
statistical analysis, of designed
      experiments, 37
statistical engineering, xiii
statistical process control, 123,
      187–188
stopper leaks case study, 82–90
  designed experiment for, 84–
      85
  multi-vari study for, 83
stratified sampling, 113, 118,
      219
success, in problem solving, 53

tablets, *see* nondisintegrating
      tablets case study
technical knowledge, 1–2
temperature, interaction with
      pressure, 22–24
testing
  overstress for low defect
      rates, 83
  problem-solving vs. product-
      acceptance-pass, 155
  running experiment, 28–29
  switching components dur-
      ing, 165

see also designed experiments;
      multi-vari studies
time-to-time variation, 8, 9, 10,
      47, 48, 62, 219
  in bore defects, 76
  in disc punch, 152
  in foundry casting porosity,
      203, 209
  in seat dimension of forged
      part, 69
  in spline demerits, 156
  in tablet disintegration, 145
tolerance analysis study, 63
total indicator reading, and mo-
      tor noise, 108–110
traditional engineering
  approach to problem solving,
      4–5
  application to eccentric discs,
      151
  vs. key variable isolation, 59,
      66–72
training
  in key variable isolation, 123
  inspectors, 105
  as solution, 113
  for statistical process control,
      123
Traver Nine-Step Problem-Solv-
      ing Process, xiv, xv
  steps, 139
type of variables, 219

unit-to-unit variation, 104
USP (United States Pharmaco-
      poeia) disintegration text,
      140

variables, 219
  determining significance, 86
  identifying those causing
      problems, 11

number in random balance
    design, 117
separating effect from resid-
    ual error, 34
variables analysis, x number of
    data points for, 117
variables isolation, xiv
variables search, 174–182, 219
    advantages of, 181
    for electronic component pull
        strength problem, 180
    for injection-molded product
        splays, 179–180
    for injection-molded product
        voids, 176–179
variation, ix–x, 2–3, 219–220
    cavity-to-cavity, 62
    day-to-day, 203
    difficulty measuring, 104
    dimensional, 62
    engine-to-engine, 171
    machine-to-machine, 48
    mold-to-mold, 203
    Pareto concept and, 115
    place-to-place, 145
    random, 115
    reading-to-reading, 131
    shift-to-shift, 48, 128, 130–131
    types of, 8–10
    unit-to-unit, 104
    within-batch, 145

within-casting, 203
    see also piece-to-piece varia-
        tion; time-to-time variation;
        within-piece variation
variation research, xiii–xiv
vendor material, *see* raw mate-
    rial
vernier caliper, 67
visual defects
    correcting, 62–64
    numerical scale for, 61
voids in injection-mold product,
    175, 220
    correcting problem, 176–179

within-batch variation, bimodal
    distribution as indicator,
    145
within-casting variation, 203
within-piece variation, 8, 9, 188,
    220
    in disc punch, 152
    in foundry cast porosity, 208–
        209
    importance of information in,
        39
    for motor noise, 104, 107
    in seat dimension, 67
    in spline demerits, 156

yields, policies and, 113